Making MORE Working Wooden Locks

Making MORE Working Wooden Locks

Complete Plans For 5 Working Wooden Locks

Tim Detweiler

Linden Publishing

Fresno CA

Making MORE Working Wooden Locks

by

Tim Detweiler

Text © 2004 by Tim Detweiler
Drawings by James Goold
Drawings © 2004 Linden Publishing

135798642

ISBN 0-941936-79-1
Printed in Singapore

Library of Congress Cataloging-in-Publication Data

Detweiler, Tim, 1931-
    Making more working wooden locks / by Tim Detweiler.
        p. cm.
    ISBN 0-941936-79-1 (alk. paper)
    1. Woodwork, 2. Wooden locks. 3. Padlocks. I. Title.
    TT200.D4798 2003
    684'.08--dc22

                                2003015263

LINDEN PUBLISHING

Linden Publishing Inc.
2006 S. Mary
Fresno, CA 93721 USA
tel 800-345-4447
www.lindenpub.com

Table of Contents

Part I:

Part II: The Projects

Part III: Gallery of Wooden Locks

Acknowledgments

I would like to thank all the wonderful people who bought my first book, *Making Working Wooden Locks*. I thank you for the phone calls and letters of compliments I have received in the past two years.

Thanks to my loyal collectors of wooden locks, Darrell Rhoades, The Hansons, Scott Crawford, the Tom Susecs, Kathy Rhoades and Robert Sykes, who have all or most of the different locks that I have made.

Thanks again to my wife, Charlene, my son, Phil, and his wife, Carlyn, for all the help in putting this book together.

— Tim Detweiler, The Lock Man

Dedication

First of all, I want to give my father much of the credit for this book. As a young boy I was never discouraged from trying to make something from wood. During the Depression in the 1930s, I learned at an early age to make do with what was available, which was not much. This helped me to learn the importance of not wasting materials. My father always said that whatever you make, make it the best you possibly can. Make it as good as if you were going to keep it for yourself.

Now I am a grandfather of wonderful twin grandsons, Erick and Matthew, who are now five years old. To them I dedicate this book with love.

Introduction

The history of locks is one of mystery and speculation. Evidence of locks and keys dates back at least 4,000 years into China, the Near East, and Egypt. Archeologists have found evidence of locks in their excavations. Some of these were forerunners of modern locks. One can only guess how advanced some of these locks must have been. Bolts on doors were common with pin tumblers that were raised by a wooden key that had matching pegs. Some of these locks were quite elaborate. As thieves became more skilled, so did the lock makers. The Romans became very skilled at making better and more secure locks of many types. Padlocks were widely used by the Romans as well as by eastern people, notably the Chinese.

This book is being produced as a way of passing on to other craftsmen a craft, that to my knowledge, no one else has ever done. This is the craft of constructing working padlocks made entirely of wood. I designed and made these locks as a challenge to myself to produce such a lock using no metal parts. In the following chapters, you will be taken step-by-step through the making of several different kinds of padlocks. We will start with the push button combination, and work up to the more challenging ones in later chapters.

First let me tell you how all this started. I was born in 1931, during the depression, about 200 miles north of Detroit, Michigan. We had very few toys in those days. A block of wood, with a little imagination, would become a bulldozer or maybe a truck. As the years passed, the toys and other projects, such as birdhouses, were made with a little more skill. In 1942 we moved to Dayton, Ohio, where in junior and senior high school I made many wooden projects in woodshop classes and also at home. I have worked in construction as a carpenter and custom homebuilder all myworking life. In 1982, I took a correspondence course in locksmithing. I worked part time at locksmithing for fourteen years before retiring in 1995. In the summer of 1988 I designed and made my first lock to sell, a warded lock. I made twenty-seven locks not knowing if I could sell even a single one. They did begin to sell, so next I designed a combination lock with a three-number combination. These locks are in my first book, *Making Working Wooden Locks* (Linden Publishing).

In November of 1988, I participated in the "Artistry in Wood" show in Dayton, Ohio to see if I could sell my wooden padlocks to the public. I not only sold locks, but also won Best of Show in woodworking for a wooden plate that I had entered into competition. For the next fourteen years, my wife and I exhibited our locks at fine art and craft shows all across the country. We have participated in over one hundred shows, and no one has disputed my claim that I am the only one making all-wooden padlocks. As of January 2003, I had made more than 3,800 wooden padlocks.

In October 1990 there was a very good article written by Dana Dunn about my locks. The article appeared in the woodworking publication, Woodshop News. In the July 1997 issue of The National Locksmith, there was an excellent article about my work by Jake Jakubrewski, who is the technical editor. This publication is distributed to locksmiths around the world. As a result, we have shipped wooden padlocks all over the United States and to at least nine foreign countries.

I hope that you will be encouraged to try your hand at making these locks. They are an excellent project for the person who wants to make something different. When you give one of these locks as a gift to a two-year-old, or a ninety-two year old, it is a joy to see their face light up and their eyes sparkle.

Materials

First let us consider the kinds of wood to be used in making a wooden lock. Almost any wood that is solid can be used for the body of the lock. I have used wood all the way from old barn boards to imported, exotic, and colorful woods, such as padauk, wenge, tiger wood, zebrawood, purpleheart, lacewood, bocote, pear, teak, and many others. I prefer hardwoods because they are much stronger and usually are more colorful. You can also use plywood to make some of the pieces. Always use good dry wood or you will have problems, such as shrinking, warping and cracking that at the very least will make it look bad, or worse: prevent the lock from working at all.

The shackles and keys must be made of good straight-grained hardwood. I use mostly ash, maple, oak, walnut and cherry.

All the keyed locks that we discuss in this book use wooden springs. This was one of my biggest problems to overcome in designing an all-wooden lock. I take extremely straight-grained ash as my first choice and hickory as a close second choice. Both woods cut well with a sharp saw, and are springy and very tough. When you have selected the woods you are going to use, lay out and make patterns if necessary for such parts as the shackle and key.

With all locks, be precise with your measurements, because that will greatly affect how the lock works. Carefully follow the step-by-step instructions. As you work on the different pieces, go slowly and trial-fit them as you proceed. When all pieces are made, clamp (do not glue) them together and try the key or the combination to make sure that the lock works properly. If you have not made wooden locks or puzzles before, I recommend that you start with the push-button combination lock on Page 14, because it is the easiest to make.

Shop Safety Tips

Shop safety is always the first concern of the craftsman. I cannot stress enough the importance of being careful. Even the most skilled and experienced craftsman can tell you stories about how they made a mistake and were either hurt or came very close to being hurt. Please keep in mind the following safety tips:

1. Never wear loose or baggy clothes. Keep shirttails tucked in, long baggy sleeves rolled up, and do not wear a necktie. If you have long hair, put it up in a cap. This is to prevent catching your clothing or hair in a tool or machine.

2. Keep your shop clean. Keep all pieces of wood out of walkways and under the workbench or in racks and boxes.

3. When you walk away from a tool or machine—turn it off.

4. Always follow the tool manufacturer's safety tips when using a tool.

5. Use sharp tools. A dull tool is far more dangerous and harder to use.

6. Dust is a major concern. Some woods are allergenic or toxic when the dust is inhaled. Wear a properly fitting facemask when sawing or sanding.

7. Ventilation of your shop is important when applying finishes. Follow instructions on the container.

8. Do not allow children in the shop.

9. If someone talks to you, stop working. The loss of attention is a certain road to injury.

Tools

You do not have to be an expert woodworker with all the latest and best tools to be successful in making a wooden lock. You can start with the tools listed under "basic" and substitute "intermediate" or "advanced" as available.

Basic Tools

1. Sharp handsaw

2. Coping saw

3. 6-inch clamps

4. Wood plane

5. Wood rasps and files

6. Brace and bits $1/4$ inch to $1 3/4$ inch

7. Carpenter's wood glue

8. Sandpaper 60 grit to 220 grit

Intermediate Tools

1. $3/8$-inch variable-speed electric drill

2. Set of $1/4$ -inch to $2 1/8$-inch Forstner-type wood bits*

3. Electric miter saw

4. Belt sander

5. Bench vise

6. Router

7. Thread box and tap for $1/2$ inch dowels

Advanced Tools

1. Table saw

2. Band saw

3. Drill press

4. Bench belt sander

5. Turning lathe

*Note—Forstner wood bits, which cut from their edge and not their center, leave a flat-bottomed hole and will make all boring much easier.

Look at tool purchases as a lifetime investment. When you buy a tool, buy the best you can afford, as it will serve you longer and better.

When drilling holes to a certain depth, use a small tape measure. Drill slowly and measure as needed to get the right depth. You can use a small stick or nail to check the depth, measuring how far it goes into the hole.

Finishing

Sanding your lock in preparation for applying the finish is a very important part of crafting a high-quality project. Start with 60-grit sandpaper for very rough surfaces and work through the available grits to the final sanding with 220-grit. Always sand with the wood grain.

Use a vacuum cleaner to remove dust from the lock, then wipe it with a tack cloth to prepare for the finish.

Much has been written about finishes in other books and articles. I will not discuss all the different finishes or how to apply them. I have used many different finishes and it is my conclusion that the best finish for a wooden lock is a good grade of polyurethane varnish. My preferred method of applying the finish is with 2-inch foam brushes, but you can use another method if you choose. However, I do not recommend that you spray the finish on, because it would get into the lock mechanism and probably ruin it. Follow directions on the finish container for best results.

About The Drawings

The projects in this book have been drawn using basic drafting techniques. Objects are drawn from three standard views: front, top, and side. These multiple views help give a clear idea of the object's structure and dimensions. Not all views are used in every drawing, only those which best illustrate the object. The drawings are shown full-size whenever possible, so you can trace them from the book and use them as plans.

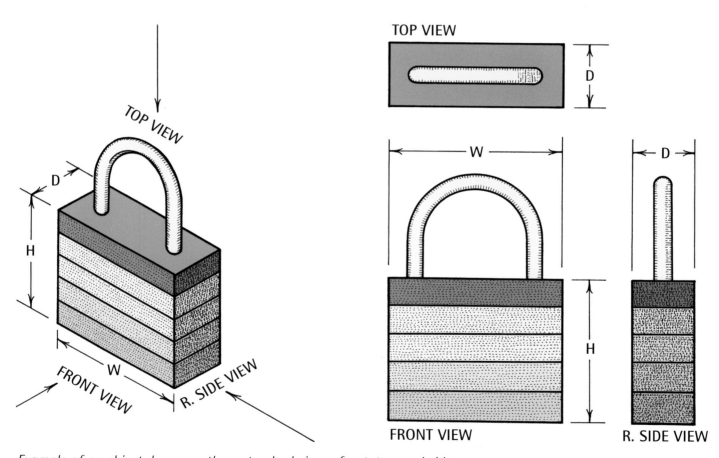

Example of an object drawn on three standard views: front, top, and side.

Photo 1: Push-Button Combination Lock

Push-Button Combination Lock

The push-button combination lock that we will make in this chapter is patterned after an antique lock that was made around 1900.

Before you start making a lock you may want to make a platform to mount on your drill press, as in Figure 1. This will help you to drill the holes precisely.

Select a piece of solid wood of your choosing for the lock body and cut it to exact size, $1^1/_2$ inches deep x $4^1/_2$ inches wide x 5 inches high (Figure 2, page 16). Do not cut to the final shape until later.

Using Figure 2 (next page), lay out the six push-button holes and the retainer-pin hole locations on the front of the lock.

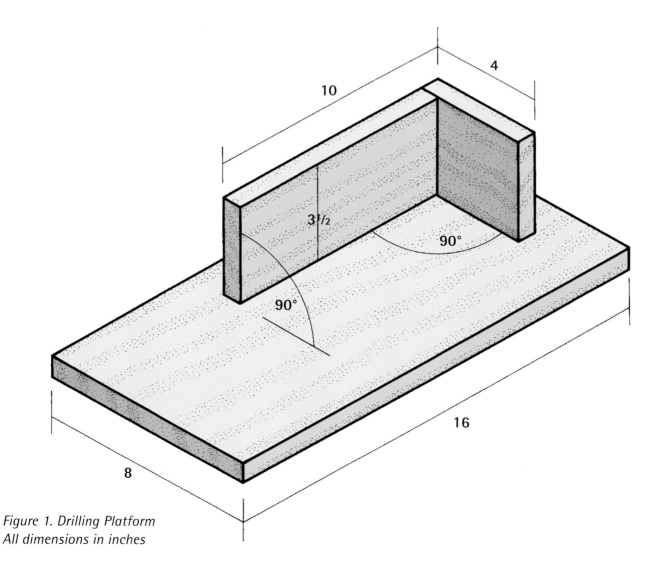

Figure 1. Drilling Platform
All dimensions in inches

Top View

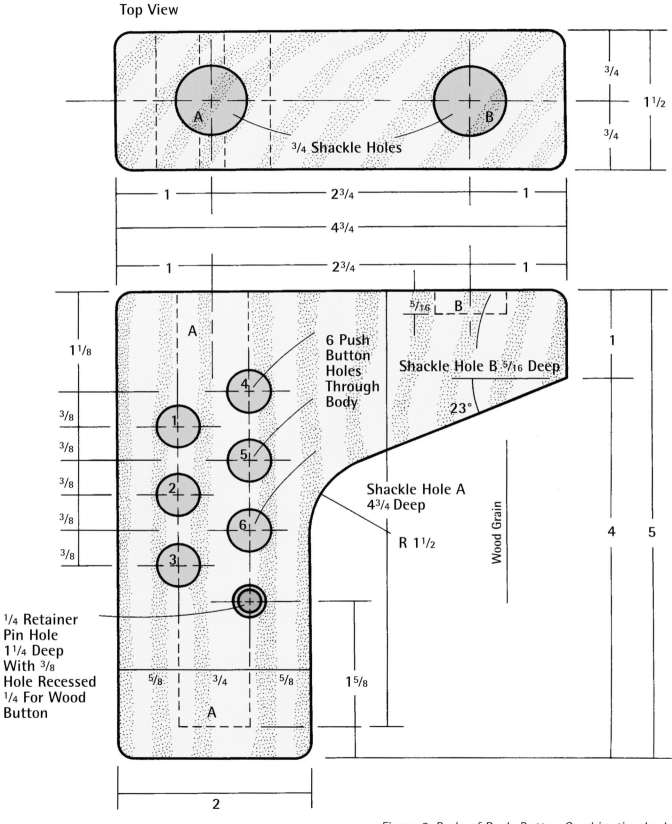

Front View

Figure 2. Body of Push-Button Combination Lock
Actual Size—all dimensions in inches

STEP # 3

Drill the six push button holes all the way through the lock body with a ¹/₂-inch drill bit. Lay the lock body on a piece of scrap wood when drilling to prevent tear out on the underside. These holes must be absolutely straight through the lock body.

STEP # 4

Use a ³/₈-inch bit to drill the retainer pin hole ¹/₄ inch deep for the wood button that will be glued in at final assembly.

STEP # 5

Drill the retainer-pin hole 1¹/₄ inch deep with a ¹/₄-inch drill bit. See Figure 2. This hole must be precise.

STEP # 6

Very carefully mark the location of the shackle holes on the top of the lock body.

STEP # 7

Set up the drilling platform and clamp the lock body in place to drill hole A exactly 4³/₄ inches deep, with a ³/₄-inch drill bit, as in Photo 2. This hole must be precisely in the center of the lock body, as shown.

STEP # 8

Reposition the lock body to drill shackle hole B. This ³/₄-inch shackle hole is bored out to a depth of ⁵/₁₆ inch.

STEP # 9

Now saw the lock body to the shape as in Figure 2 and Photo 3. Sand all saw marks and other rough places smooth to prepare for rounding the edges over.

STEP # 10

Use a ¹/₄-inch or ⁵/₁₆-inch round-over bit, if you have one, in your router to round all corners per Figure 2 and Photo 3. If you do not have a router, the corners can be rounded by hand. Wait until all pieces are made and fitted before you do the final sanding.

Photo 2: Drilling Shackle Hole

Photo 3: Lock Body Ready to Sand

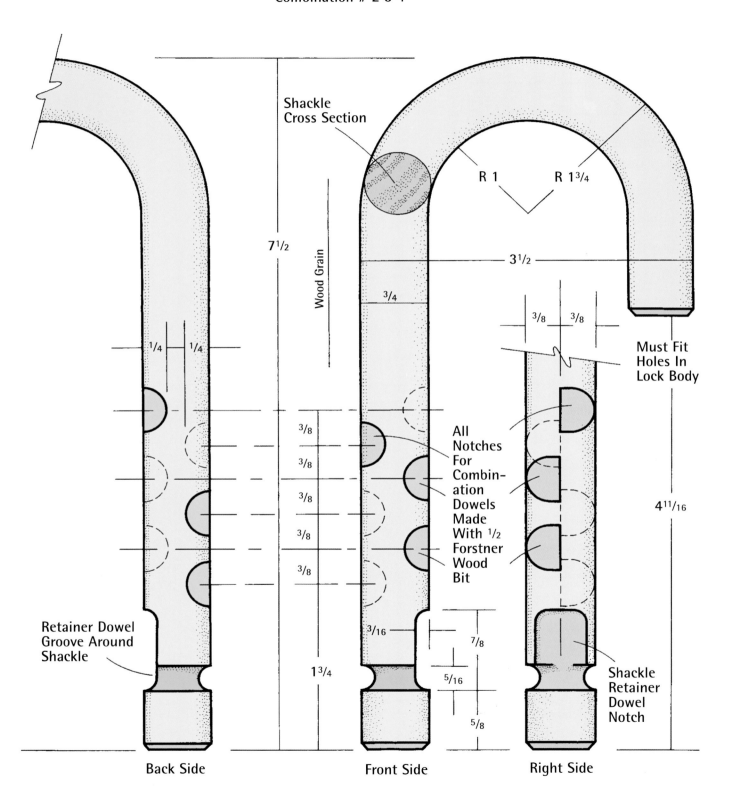

Shackle
Combination # 2 3 4

Shackle
Cross Section

7¹/₂

Wood Grain

³/₄

R 1   R 1³/₄

3¹/₂

³/₈ ³/₈

¹/₄ ¹/₄

Must Fit
Holes In
Lock Body

³/₈

³/₈

All
Notches
For
Combin-
ation
Dowels
Made
With ¹/₂
Forstner
Wood
Bit

³/₈

³/₈

4¹¹/₁₆

³/₈

³/₈

Retainer Dowel
Groove Around
Shackle

³/₁₆

⁷/₈

1³/₄

⁵/₁₆

⁵/₈

Shackle
Retainer
Dowel
Notch

Back Side   Front Side   Right Side

Figure 3. Shackle for Push-Button Combination Lock.
Actual Size—all dimensions in inches

Photo 4: Shackle Rounded Over, Not Cut to Length

STEP #11

The shackle (Figure 3) is probably the most difficult part to make. Select a piece of straight-grained wood $3/4$ inches thick, $3^1/_2$ inches wide and approximately 10 inches long. White pine is the easiest wood to work with but is not very strong. I recommend a good hardwood for the shackle, though it is somewhat harder to work with. Remember to proceed carefully, because the shackle hole is exactly $3/4$ inches in diameter. The final shackle will be approximately $^1/_{16}$ inch smaller than the hole. It must move up and down as well as freely turn 360°.

Very carefully lay out the shackle outline (Figure 3) on the wood to make a pattern. The notching will be done after the shackle is rounded and fitted into the lock. The final width of the shackle must be just a little less than the distance across the shackle holes in the lock body (probably a total width of $3^7/_{16}$ inches).

The shackle can be any height you like. This will only affect how the lock looks not how it works. May I suggest that you make the shackle ends 2 inches or 3 inches longer than you want the finished shackle? The reason for this is, you can leave the extra length square so that you will be able to clamp it down, making it easier to hold while rounding over.

STEP #12

After cutting out the shackle, sand the saw marks off and sand all surfaces down so that the $3/4$ inch thickness is now $^1/_{32}$-inch undersized. This will help when the final fitting is done. If you have a router and a $3/8$ - inch round-over bit, rounding over will be much easier. Be very careful and take two or three passes to round the shackle over. Then remove the extra length from the shackle (Photo 4). This will allow you to finish the rounding over and sanding to fit into the shackle holes. Make sure both ends of the shackle hit the bottom of their holes.

STEP #13

When you are finished sanding the shackle, lay out the shackle retainer dowel groove that goes all the way around the shackle $5/8$ inch from the bottom (Figure 3). This notch can be made square instead of round if you prefer. Cut or carve this groove approximately $^3/_{16}$ inches deep and $^5/_{16}$ inches wide. Find a $^1/_4$ inch x 3 inch dowel that will just slip into the retainer-dowel hole in the lock body. You may have to sand the dowel a little.

Now insert the shackle partway until the dowel goes into the hole all the way. If the dowel hits the shackle or rubs on it when the shackle is turned, remove more from the groove until it rotates freely.

Photo 5: Shackle Notched and Ready to Finish

Lay out the shackle retainer-dowel notch just above the groove. This notch is cut to the same depth as the groove. The shackle must move freely up and down and rotate 360° without binding.

Make the notch in the shackle for the combination buttons or dowels. Now you will understand why the shackle hole in the lock body must be in the exact center, as shown in Figure 2.

Place the shackle in the lock body and use the drilling platform to position the lock for drilling the six combination dowel holes. Use a 1/2-inch Forstner bit, and set the depth to precisely drill half-way into the shackle, as shown in Figure 3, right-side view. Please note that the holes are placed to result in the unlocking combination of buttons 2, 3 and 4 being pushed flush with the front of the lock, with 1, 5, and 6 pushed flush with the back of the lock.

Drilling the notches in the shackle when it is in the lock body it ensures that they all line up properly. Drill one hole and pull the shackle out of the lock body to clear out the sawdust and chips. Now drill the other notches following the same procedure (Photo 5).

If you want to make a different combination just drill the notches in the shackle in another order, making sure you drill from the front or back of the lock in different holes. Be careful not to drill the same hole from both the front and back of the shackle.

Make six combination buttons from 1/2-inch dowels as in Figure 4. Before you saw the length of the buttons try to pass the dowel through the buttonholes in the lock body. The dowel must slide freely and have a little play.

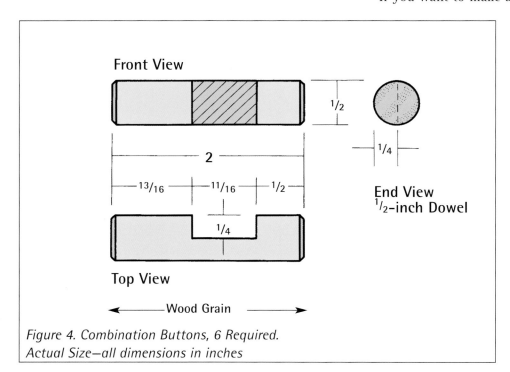

Front View

2

13/16   11/16   1/2

1/2

1/4

1/4

End View
1/2-inch Dowel

Top View

◀—— Wood Grain ——▶

Figure 4. Combination Buttons, 6 Required.
Actual Size—all dimensions in inches

Sand the dowel as needed to free it up. Now cut the dowel into six 2-inch pieces and notch as shown in Figure 4.

STEP #17

Fit combination dowel #4 first, see Figure 2. Start the shackle into the shackle hole and at the same time slip #4 dowel into #4 hole, in position to let the shackle slide past. Slide the shackle all the way into the lock body. If you have the #4 dowel turned the right way you can lock the lock with just this one dowel. The dowel should be flush with the face of the lock when unlocked. If the combination dowel #4 binds or pushes hard, you must carefully sand or carve a little off where it is binding. When it works properly, proceed to dowel #1 and repeat the steps to fit it to the lock. Then proceed down in this order: 5, 2, 6, and 3, for the other combination dowels.

STEP #18

Now sand all parts of the lock carefully with the wood grain. Round all edges and corners slightly, except the notches in the combination dowels.

STEP #19

Number each combination dowel with a number punch, wood-burner, or a painted on number. Remember the combination is 2, 3, 4.

STEP #20

Prepare a place to hang or lay each piece of the lock to dry after the finish is applied. Clean all parts with a vacuum cleaner and wipe with a tack cloth to prepare for the finish.

STEP #21

I like to use polyurethane finish on my locks as it goes on easily and makes a hard and durable finish.

My favorite method of application is a 2-inch foam brush. You may use other finishes if you like. I do not use a spray finish because it can get into some locks and cause problems. Don't forget to finish a $3/8$ inch wood button for the retainer-pin hole.

I use two coats of finish on most locks. After the first coat is dry, sand with very fine sandpaper or no. 4 steel wool to remove any roughness. Clean with a vacuum cleaner and wipe down with a tack cloth. You may want to apply a third coat of finish to produce a real professional job.

STEP #22

Assemble the lock as described in Step #17. Then cut a piece of $1/4$-inch dowel 1 inch long from the temporary dowel pin used in Step #13. Put a small drop of glue on the end of the dowel and push it all the way into the lock. Now carefully glue the wood button into the recess over the retainer pin.

Congratulations! You have completed a working push-button combination lock. I hope you enjoyed this project and will build the other locks in this book.

Photo 6A: Chinese Lock and Key

Photo 6B: Chinese Lock Open

Chinese Lock

The Chinese lock is very old, perhaps several hundred years since it was first made in China. Some of these locks were made to look like a dog or some other animal. Other locks were made in the shape of fish. The lock in this chapter is the same shape as, and works the same way as a brass padlock on a wooden box that I have. The box holds a hand-carved ivory chess set. I carved a big horned ram from walnut and traded it for the chess set in 1961.

The kind of wood you use is for you to decide. I have used pine, which makes a nice lock, but some of the hardwoods make a stronger and more colorful lock. Study the plans and instructions before starting to work on the lock.

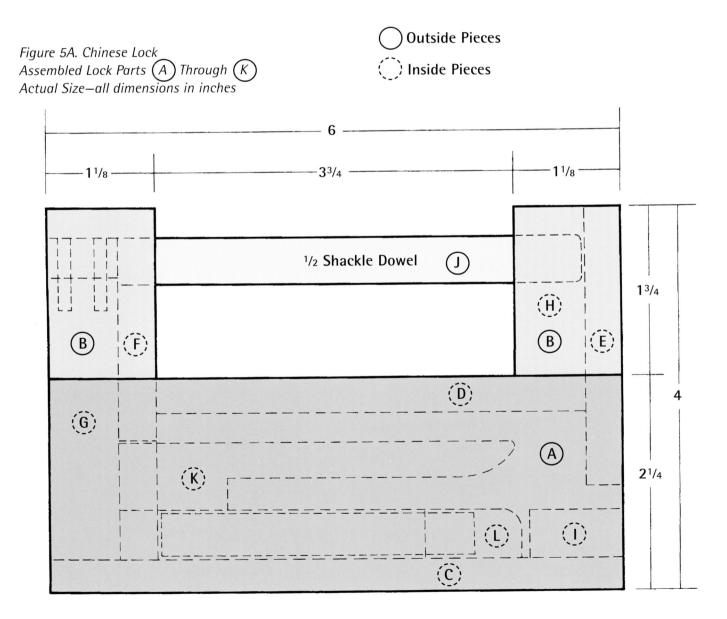

Figure 5A. Chinese Lock Assembled Lock Parts (A) Through (K) Actual Size—all dimensions in inches

◯ **Outside Pieces**

◌ **Inside Pieces**

Front View

Figure 5B. Chinese Lock
Actual Size—all dimensions in inches

Top View

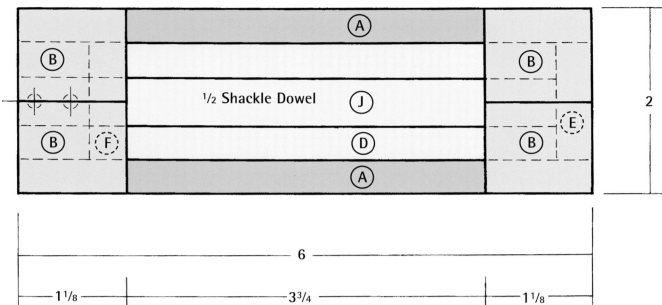

Figure 6. Chinese Lock
Actual Size—all dimensions in inches

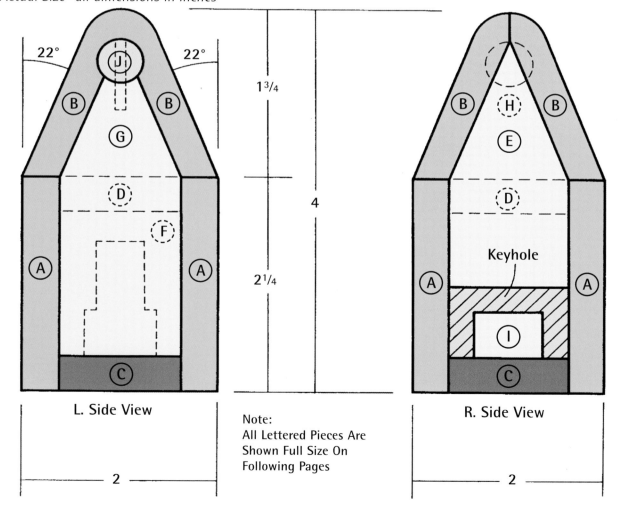

L. Side View

R. Side View

Note:
All Lettered Pieces Are
Shown Full Size On
Following Pages

STEP #1

Lay out parts A through F on 3/8 inch thick wood. Make sure the wood grain is running in the correct direction.

Use Figure 7 through 12 (next page) to make the pieces. Be precise in your layout and cutting of each piece. The more precise you are the less you will have to fit the pieces as the lock is glued together.

STEP #2

Use 3/4 inch thick wood to make pieces G, H, and I as shown in Figures 13, 14, and 15.

(Figures 13, 14, 15)

Drill a 1/4 inch hole 3/8 inch deep in the backside of part G, as shown in Figure 13.

Please note that piece I, Figure 15 has a finished width of 11/16 inches.

Figure 7. Lock Sides (A) *2 Required*
Actual Size—all dimensions in inches

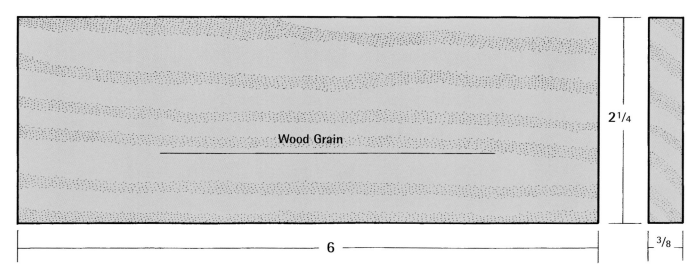

Figure 8. Lock Roof (B) *4 Required*
Actual Size—all dimensions in inches

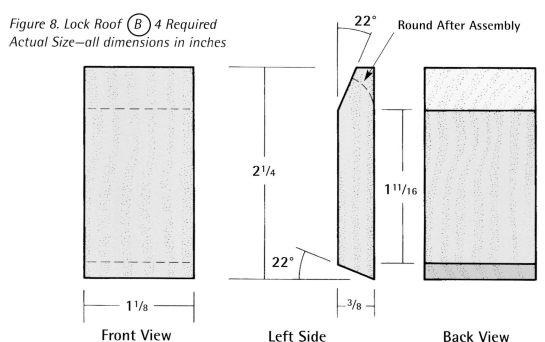

Front View   **Left Side**   **Back View**

Figure 9. (C) *Lock Bottom*
Actual Size—all dimensions in inches

End View

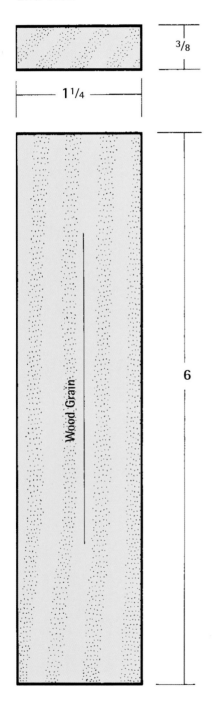

Top View

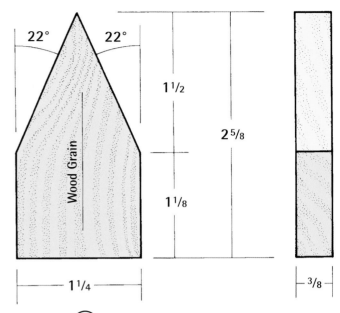

Figure 11. (E) *Right Side*
Actual Size—all dimensions in inches

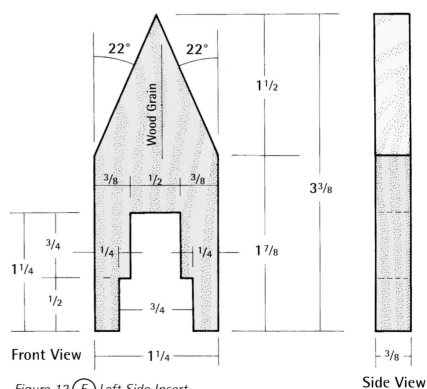

Front View

Side View

Figure 12. (F) *Left Side Insert*
Actual Size—all dimensions in inches

Figure 10. (D) Lock Body Top
Actual Size—all dimensions in inches

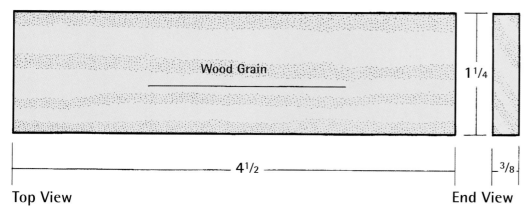

Wood Grain

$1^1/4$

$4^1/2$

$3/8$

Top View　　　　　　　　　　　　　　　**End View**

Figure 14. (H) Filler Piece
Actual Size—all dimensions in inches

Figure 13. (G) Shackle End Piece
Actual Size—all dimensions in inches

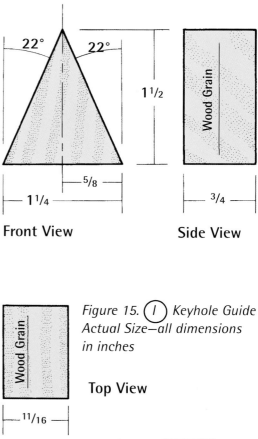

22°　　22°

$1^1/2$

Wood Grain

$5/8$

$1^1/4$

$3/4$

Front View　　　　　　**Side View**

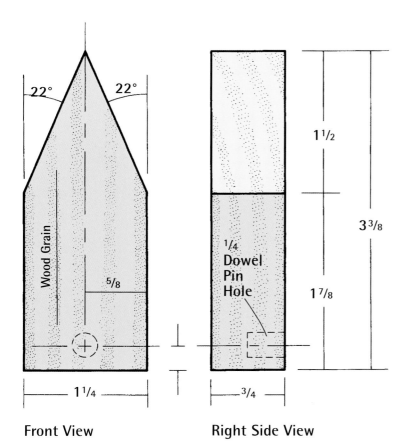

22°　　　22°

Wood Grain

$5/8$

$1/4$
**Dowel
Pin
Hole**

$1^1/2$

$3^3/8$

$1^7/8$

$1^1/4$　　　　　$3/4$

Front View　　　　**Right Side View**

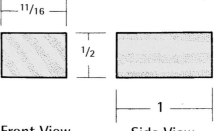

Figure 15. (I) Keyhole Guide
Actual Size—all dimensions
in inches

Wood Grain

Top View

$^{11}/16$

$1/2$

1

Front View　　　**Side View**

Photo 7: Trial Fit of Lock Body Parts

Photo 8: Pieces E and B

STEP #3

Gluing the lock body together.

Take the two sides A, bottom C and top D and trial fit them together. Place E and F in position and check all joints and fit them as needed. Temporarily wrap a rubber band around this assembly to hold it together or clamp as shown in Photo 7.

STEP #4

Place the B pieces on the top of this assembly to check their fit, as in Figures 5 and 6.

Glue two B pieces to the E piece. Do not glue to the sides A at this time (Photo 8).

Now glue two B pieces to the F piece, but not to the sides A at this time (Photo 9).

STEP #5

When the glue is dry, fit piece H into place with piece E and then glue it to the B-E assembly, but not to the top D piece. *Note* This assembly must be free so it can be bored out for the shackle dowel part J, before it is glued into place in the lock body.

STEP #6

Remove assembly B-F and fit part G into place, as in Figures 5 and 6.

Clamp assembly B-F and piece G together. Use a 1/2 inch Forstner drill bit to drill a hole all the way through this assembly absolutely straight and square with the face of part G where the parts B come to a point at the top. See Figure 6 to get the location of this hole. It is imperative that the pieces do not move during the drilling of this hole (Photo 10).

STEP #7

Now take assembly B-E-H and drill a ¹/₂ inch hole exactly ³/₄ inches deep into the H side. See Figure 6 for location of this hole. This hole also must be straight and square with the H side of this assembly. This shackle hole must be aligned with the other shackle hole.

STEP #8

Cut a piece of ¹/₂ inch dowel J, 5⁵/₈ inches long. Fit it into the notch cut in the top of part G in Step #6.

Look at Figure 16 to see how two small dowels are used to secure the ¹/₂ -inch shackle dowel J in place. When fitted and drilled, glue in place on part G as shown in Figure 16.

STEP #9

Now glue the lock body together. There is no set order in gluing the pieces together, so proceed carefully and try not to get any glue on the wood where it will show after assembly. If you have a few edges or corners that do not quite match up, they can be sanded off later. Carefully round over the tops of the B pieces as in Figure 6.

STEP #10

Finish sanding piece I, Figures 5 and 6, and glue into place.

STEP #11

Slide the shackle into the lock if you can. You will probably have to do some sanding and fitting to make a nice fit. After the locking slide assembly K-L is made and attached, it will slide in easier.

Photo 9: Pieces E and F

Photo 10: Drilling Shackle Hole in B, F, G Assembly

Photo 11: Assembled Shackle

STEP #12

The locking slide, Figures 16 and 17 and Photo 11, consists of parts K and L. Use a piece of wood ¹/₂ inch x ¹¹/₁₆ inch x 4 inches to make part K: Cut to the shape in Figure 16 and sand the ¹/₂ inch dimension to about ¹⁵/₃₂ inches so that it slides through the top part of the hole in part F.

Now make the locking slide Figure 17 from ¹/₂ inch wood. The dimensions shown are finish size after sanding. Carefully layout the notches for the springs and the 5 degree angle of the cutout in each side. The spring notches should be ¹/₁₆ inch to fit the two wood springs.

Drill a ¹/₄ inch hole ³/₈ inches into the exact center of the left end of the locking slide, see Figure 17.

Figure 16. Shackle Assembly
Actual Size—all dimensions in inches

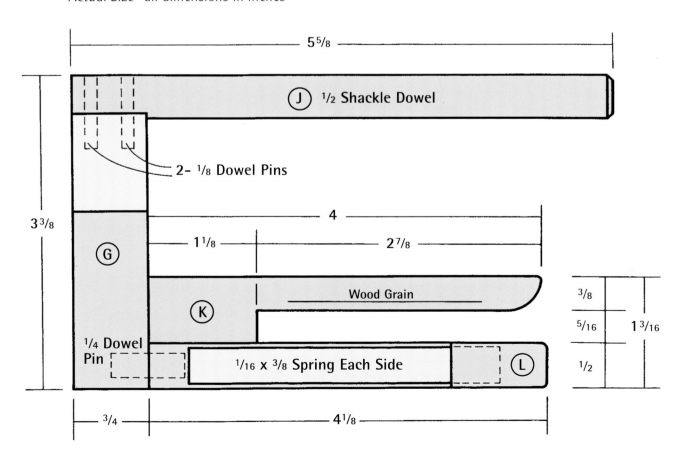

Side View

STEP #13

Make two wood springs, Figure 18, from straight-grained ash or hickory. Fit them into the notches in the locking slide. Glue them with just a small bead of glue in the notches. Place them, as shown in Figure 17, so they will not protrude above or below the slide. The springs, when compressed, must fit behind the notches on the left or free end of the springs.

STEP #14

Glue part K in the center on top of the locking slide and flush with the left end of L. See Figure 16 and 17.

STEP #15

Cut a ¼ inch dowel about ¾ inche long to fit in the dowel pinhole, Figures 16 and 17. Fit the slide onto part G of the shackle and glue in place. Slide the shackle only part way into the lock to check the fit. Do not slide it all the way in, or you may have a problem if the lock snaps shut. Wait until you have the key fitted to the lock before you close the lock.

Figure 18. Wood Spring, 2 Required
Actual Size—all dimensions in inches

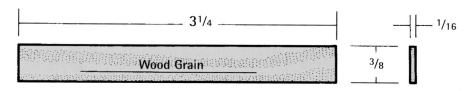

Figure 17. Ⓛ Locking Slide
Actual Size—all dimensions in inches

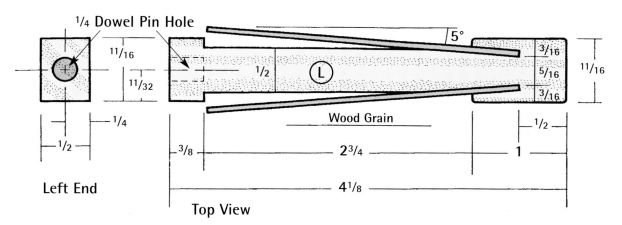

Figure 19. Key
Actual Size—all dimensions in inches

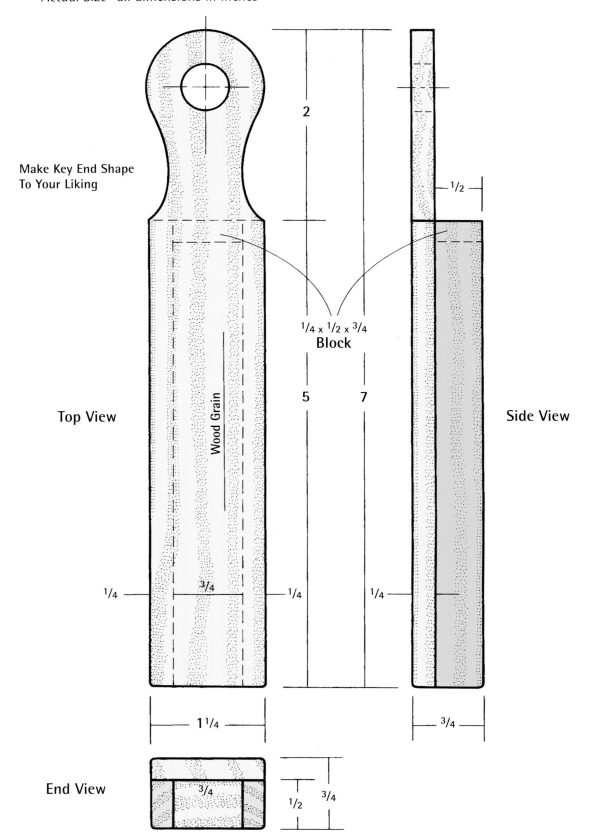

Make Key End Shape
To Your Liking

2

1/4 x 1/2 x 3/4
Block

Wood Grain

5   7

Top View

Side View

1/4   3/4   1/4   1/4

1 1/4   3/4

End View   3/4

1/2   3/4

STEP #16 THE KEY

Make the key (Figure 19) from ¹/₄ inch wood. Sand smooth and glue together. Please note that you can make the bow end of the key some other shape if you prefer.

When the glue is dry, try to insert the key into the keyhole. You probably will have to sand the width and the height of the key a little. Check the fit as you sand so that there is about ¹/₁₆ inch clearance in width and height.

Now take the shackle and carefully slip the key into place on the shackle. The key must slip onto the shackle without extra force while pushing the springs into the cutouts in the locking slide. You may have to do a little fitting to make it work properly. When it does work, slide the shackle into the lock. It should lock with a nice snap. At this time, you may have to sand or file the slide, the end of the shackle or the shackle hole to make the lock work, as it should.

Photo 12: Key

STEP #17

Sand all parts of the lock and key with the wood grain to a final sanding with 220-grit paper. Round all edges slightly.

STEP #18

Prepare the lock and key for finish by cleaning it with a vacuum cleaner and wiping it off with a tack cloth.

You can use polyurethane finish or most other finishes on this lock. If you want, you can use a spray finish. Use several light coats of finish, sanding lightly and cleaning between coats.

I hope you enjoyed making this lock and will make the others in this book.

Chinese Lock with Key

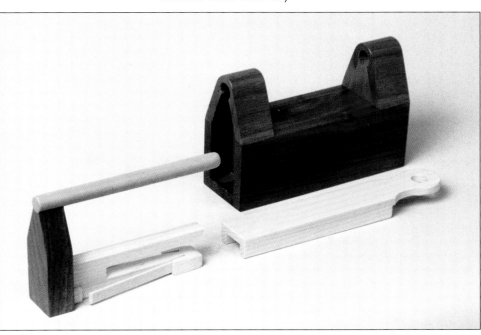

Screw Key Lock

Screw key locks are very old. I do not know when they were first made. The lock in this chapter is made to look and work like an old lock that I have. Like most of these old locks, mine was made around 1900. Most of these old locks were made of forged steel. The locks are heavy and very strong.

Please note, before you consider making this lock, you must have access to a turning lathe, the means of cutting threads on a 1/2 inch dowel, and a matching tap to make the threads inside the lock.

Study the drawings (Figure 20) and step-by-step instructions carefully before you begin making the lock.

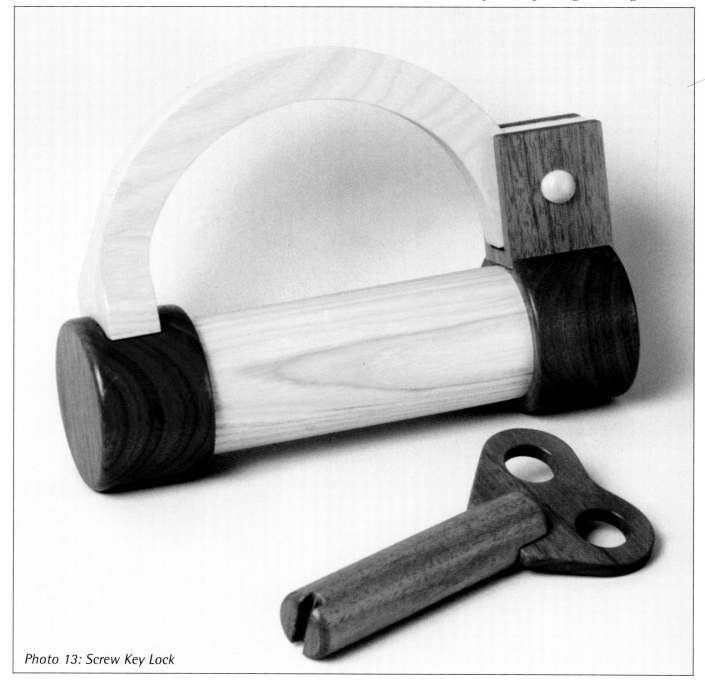

Photo 13: Screw Key Lock

Figure 20. Screw Key Lock, Cut-Away View
Parts (A) Through (G)
Actual Size—all dimensions in inches

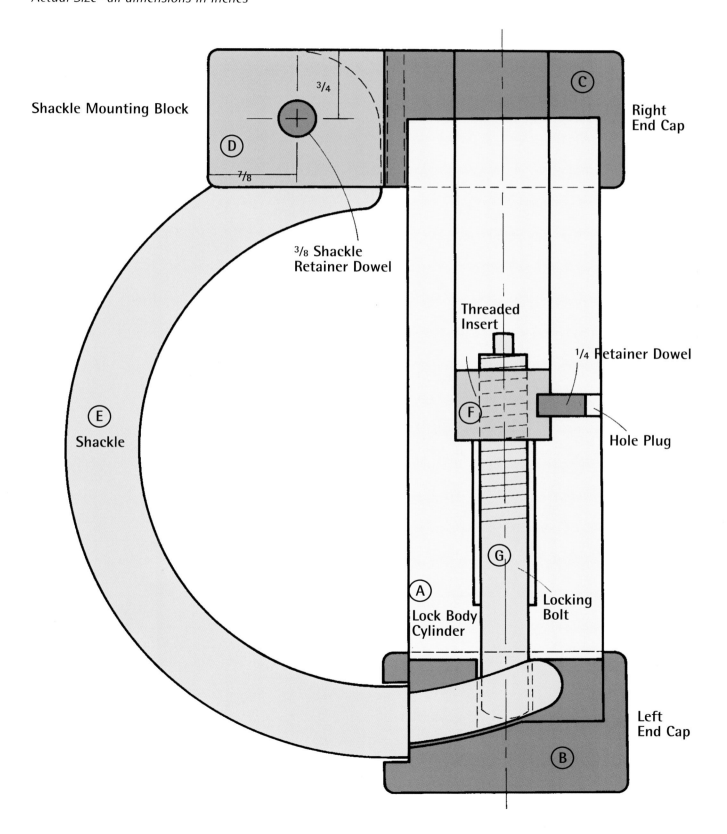

Shackle Mounting Block

3/4

7/8

(D)

(C)

Right End Cap

3/8 **Shackle Retainer Dowel**

Threaded Insert

1/4 **Retainer Dowel**

(F)

(E)
Shackle

Hole Plug

(G)

(A)
Lock Body Cylinder

Locking Bolt

Left End Cap

(B)

Figure 21. (A) *Lock Body Cylinder*
Actual Size—all dimensions in inches

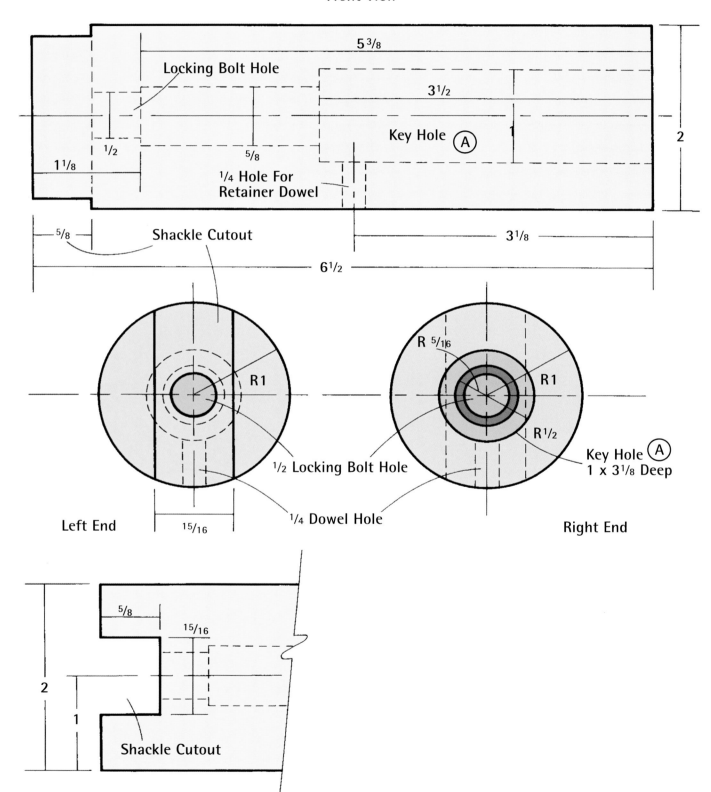

Front View

5 3/8

Locking Bolt Hole

3 1/2

Key Hole (A)

1

2

1/2

5/8

1 1/8

1/4 Hole For
Retainer Dowel

5/8   Shackle Cutout

3 1/8

6 1/2

R1

R 5/16

R1

R 1/2

1/2 Locking Bolt Hole

Key Hole (A)
1 x 3 1/8 Deep

Left End   15/16   1/4 Dowel Hole   Right End

5/8

15/16

2

1

Shackle Cutout

Top View of Left End

STEP #1

Select the wood of your choice, but I strongly recommend hardwoods, especially for the shackle. Use contrasting woods for some of the parts for a more attractive lock.

STEP #2

Making the lock body cylinder A, Figure 21. To make the body cylinder, you can use a solid piece of wood or glue-laminate pieces together, as long as you can get the 2-inch diameter and 6 1/2-inch length required for the finished size.

After you turn the cylinder to size and sand it to the final size proceed to Step #3. Do not notch or drill out the interior until later.

STEP #3

Figure 22 shows the finished size of the left end cap B. Saw a round piece of wood 2 3/4 inches in diameter and 1 5/8 inches thick. This will give you extra wood to work with when turning on the lathe. Mount this block on a piece of 3/4 inch wood by first gluing a piece of cardboard, such as a piece from the back of a writing tablet, to this piece and then glue the end cap to the cardboard and clamp. This will enable you to separate them after turning without marring the end cap. Find the exact center of the end cap and mount it to a faceplate. You must have a finished diameter of 2 1/2 inches and a thickness of 1 1/2 inches.

Figure 22. (B) *Left End Cap*
Actual Size—all dimensions in inches

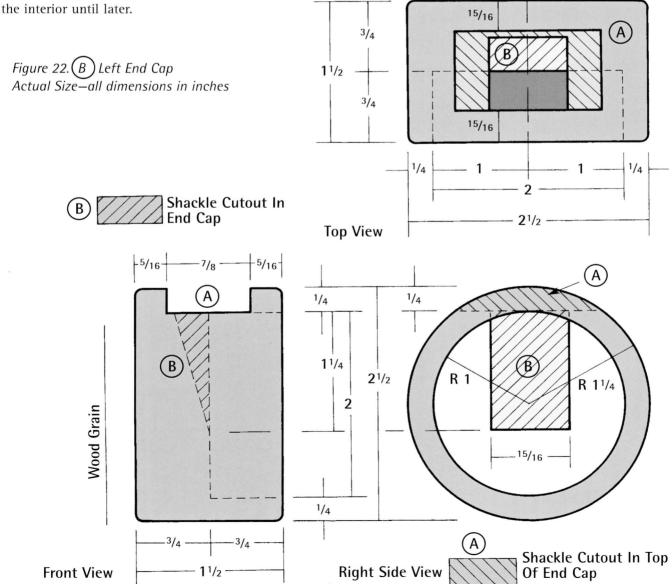

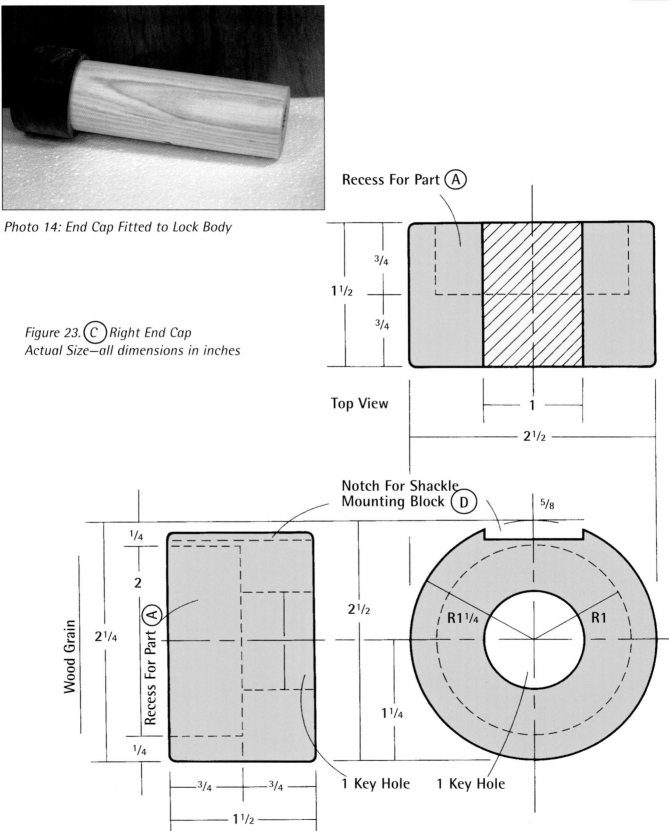

Photo 14: End Cap Fitted to Lock Body

Figure 23. (C) Right End Cap
Actual Size—all dimensions in inches

Recess For Part (A)

3/4

1 1/2

3/4

Top View

1

2 1/2

Notch For Shackle
Mounting Block (D)

5/8

1/4

2

Recess For Part (A)

2 1/4

Wood Grain

1/4

3/4   3/4

1 1/2

2 1/2

1 1/4

R1 1/4   R1

1 Key Hole   1 Key Hole

Front View

Right Side View

STEP #4

When the glue has set, place on the lathe and turn the outside to size. Then start to cut the recess for the lock body cylinder. Mark one end of the lock body as the left end. Now very carefully cut out the recess exactly 3/4 inch deep and just wide enough to accept the lock body. You want this to be a very nice fit. Make it just loose enough to allow a little glue into the assembly later on. Round over the edges slightly and sand with 220-grit sandpaper.

To remove the end cap from the turning block use a large chisel placed so that it will not mar the end cap, and tap it with a hammer to separate the end cap from the turning block by splitting the cardboard. Now sand off the cardboard that is on the end cap and round the edge slightly. Mark this end cap for the left end of the lock. We will notch and fit it to the lock body later.

Photo 15: Drilling Key Hole in Lock Body

STEP #5

Make the right end cap C, Figure 23, using Steps 3 and 4. The right end cap is exactly the same as the left end cap except for the notches etc., which we will make later.

STEP #6

The most critical part of making this lock is the drilling of the holes in each end of the lock body cylinder. You must drill all holes precisely straight and in the center. See Figure 21 and drill the holes in the following order.

Clamp the body cylinder to the drill platform, Figure 21, right end up, being careful not to damage the cylinder. Use padding to protect the cylinder. The lock cylinder must be perfectly parallel with the drill bit. The drill bit must hit in the exact center of the lock body cylinder (Photo 15).

STEP #7

Use a 1 inch Forstner bit if you have one, or you can use a brad point bit to drill the key hole A, Figure 21, exactly 3½ inches into the body cylinder.

Photo 16: Completed End Cap B

Photo 17: Completed End Cap C

STEP # 8

Do not move the body cylinder. Remove the 1 inch drill bit and replace it with a ⅝ inch drill bit. Now drill farther into the body cylinder to a depth of approximately 5⅜ inches. See Figure 21.

STEP # 9

Remove the body cylinder from the drill platform and turn the left end up and reclamp it as before. Use a ½ inch drill to drill the locking bolt hole exactly in the center of the cylinder. See Figure 21. Drill all the way into the ⅝ inch hole that was drilled from the right end of the body cylinder.

STEP # 10

Use Figure 21 to layout the shackle cutout on the left end of the lock body cylinder. Note that the depth of the cutout is ⅝ inch. This is important as the end cap only covers ¾ inch of the body cylinder. Note how the wood grain runs and plan ahead for the way you want the lock to look when assembled. The end caps will have the wood grain running vertical. Carefully cut the notch.

STEP # 11

Lay out the shackle cutout A in Figure 22 on the left end cap. Make this cut across the end grain as shown. Be very careful sawing this notch, you do not want to have to make another end cap.

STEP # 12

Use Figure 22 and lay out the shackle cutout B. Use a small chisel to cut out this notch. You probably will have to do a little fitting later (Photo 16).

STEP # 13

Now lay out notch D for the shackle mounting block, on the right end cap, Figure 23. Cut this notch on the end grain side as you did with the left end cap. Be sure to make the notch straight and flat on the bottom.

STEP #14

Lay out the exact center of the right end cap C. Drill the 1 inch keyhole all the way through. See Figure 23. This hole must line up with the keyhole in lock body A. You may have to file and sand it out a little. This hole must be large enough to accept the 1 inch dowel of the key without binding when the key is inserted and turned (Photo 17).

STEP #15

Make the shackle mounting block D, using Figure 24. This block must fit the notch made in the top of the right end cap, Figure 23. If it is a little over 1 inch

Figure 24. (D) Shackle Mounting Block
Actual Size—all dimensions in inches

thick, make the notch in the end cap bigger to fit it. Just make sure the notch is centered in the end cap.

Use a ³/₈ inch bit to drill the shackle retainer dowel hole perfectly straight and square through the shackle-mounting block (Photo 18).

STEP #16

Lay out the shackle using Figure 25 on a piece of ¹/₂ inch hardwood or you may use plywood if you would like. The plywood would be much stronger, but not as attractive.

Saw out the shackle leaving just enough extra wood for sanding. Do not drill the locking bolt hole now.

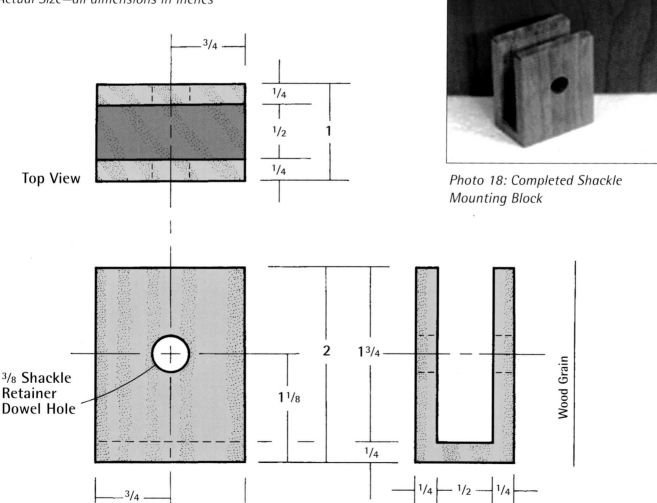

Photo 18: Completed Shackle Mounting Block

Top View

³/₄
¹/₄
¹/₂
¹/₄
1

³/₈ **Shackle Retainer Dowel Hole**

2
1³/₄
1¹/₈
¹/₄

³/₄
1¹/₂

¹/₄ — ¹/₂ — ¹/₄
1

Wood Grain

Front View   **Right Side View**

Figure 25. (E) *Shackle*
Actual Size—all dimensions in inches

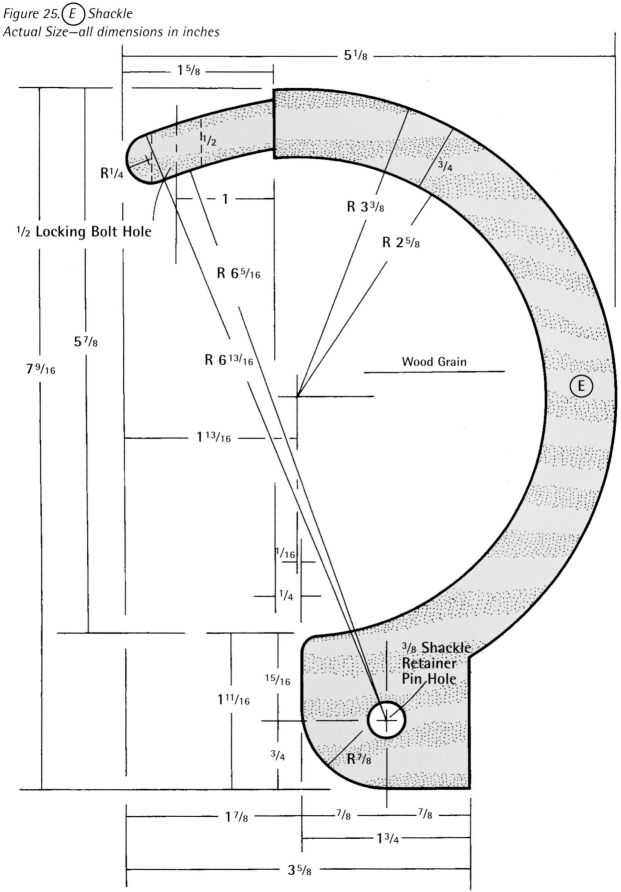

5 1/8

1 5/8

1/2

R 1/4

1

3/4

R 3 3/8

1/2 **Locking Bolt Hole**

R 2 5/8

R 6 5/16

R 6 13/16

Wood Grain

5 7/8

7 9/16

1 13/16

(E)

1/16

1/4

3/8 **Shackle**
Retainer
Pin Hole

15/16

1 11/16

R 7/8

3/4

1 7/8   7/8   7/8

1 3/4

3 5/8

Insert a ¼ inch dowel into the hole, mark it at the outside surface of the lock body. Remove the dowel and cut off ¼ inch shorter than the mark. Place a drop of glue on the end of the dowel and push it all the way into the hole.

The ¼ inch deep hole that is left is to be filled with a plug made of the same wood as the lock body. After the plug is glued in place, sand it off flush with the surface.

STEP #32

The key should now extend and retract the locking bolt freely. Use the key to back the locking bolt back into the lock body. It should be about flush with the hole in the left end of the lock body.

Now take all pieces not glued together apart and finish sanding all surfaces that will be exposed after final assembly. Round all exposed edges to suite your requirements for looks and feel.

STEP #33

When all sanding is completed, assemble the lock as you did before. Line up the end cap C with the shackle in place. Slide end cap B on the lock body and check the alignment of the shackle to make sure it goes into place. Now make a very small mark on the lock body and the end cap at each end to show the position when they are glued in place. Remove the shackle for now.

STEP #34

Spread a little glue inside end cap C where it comes in contact with the lock body and slide into place at the mark made on the body.

Next glue the end cap B into place using the same procedure.

STEP #35

Temporarily install the shackle again. Now use the key to see if the locking bolt goes into the hole in the shackle. You may have to enlarge the hole in the shackle a little to make the lock work properly.

STEP # 3 6

Remove the shackle to prepare for applying the finish. Select two ³/₈ inch wood buttons to use in the shackle pivot pinholes after finish is applied.

Clean all parts with a vacuum cleaner and wipe with a tack cloth.

Apply at least two coats of finish to your lock, sanding and cleaning between each coat. Brush with the grain where possible and do not let the finish run.

STEP # 3 7

When your finish is completely dry, glue one of the wood buttons in one side of the shackle-mounting block.

Insert a ³/₈ inch dowel in the pivot hole, mark at the surface and cut ¹/₈ inch shorter than the mark. This dowel must pass easily through the hole in the shackle.

Place the shackle in position, put a small bead of glue on one end of the ³/₈ inch dowel pin and push all the way into the pivot hole. Put a little glue around the edge of the buttonhole and tap the second wood button into place.

You have just completed one of the more difficult locks I have made. I have made 26 of them to date. You can be proud of your lock. It is truly a showpiece of your skill. Sign and date your lock so it can always be identified as one of your projects.

The completed screw-key lock

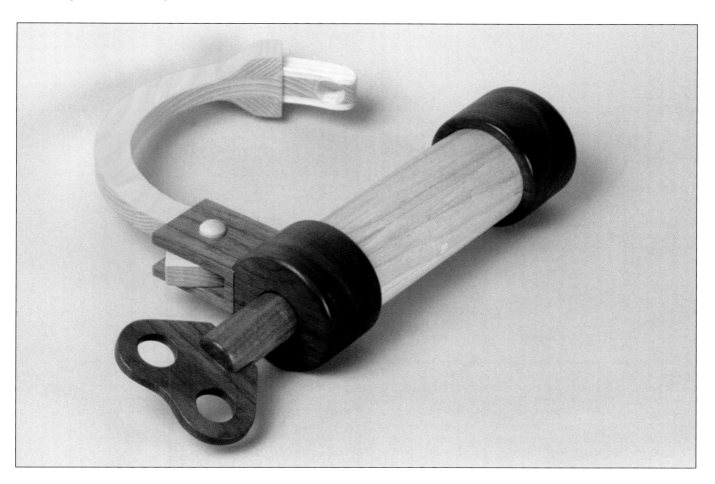

Figure 29. Giant Antique Lever Lock
Lock Parts (A) Through (E)
1/2 Actual Size—all dimensions in inches

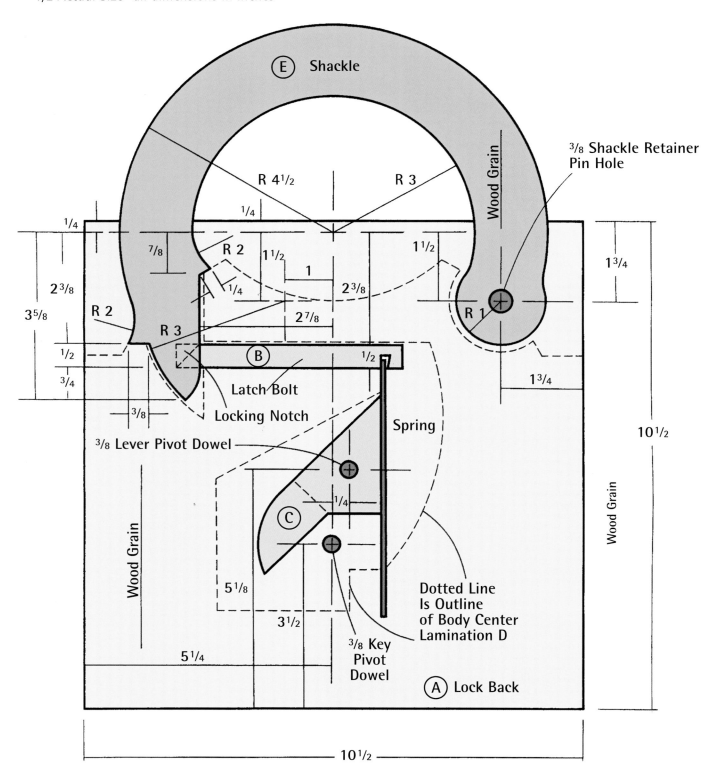

Giant Antique Lever Lock

These locks date back at least 150 years. They were made of wrought iron and were often used on smoke house doors. Lock collectors now often call them "smokies." Lever locks are still made today. Some of these locks are used in high security applications.

The lock we will make in this chapter is about 15 inches high and is almost identical to the third lock that I made 20 years ago.

Read the instructions and study the drawings carefully before you start to work on the lock. Note: Figures 29, 30, and 31 are drawn one half actual size.

Photo 22: Giant Antique Lever Lock

Figure 30. Lock Face
1/2 Actual Size—all dimensions in inches

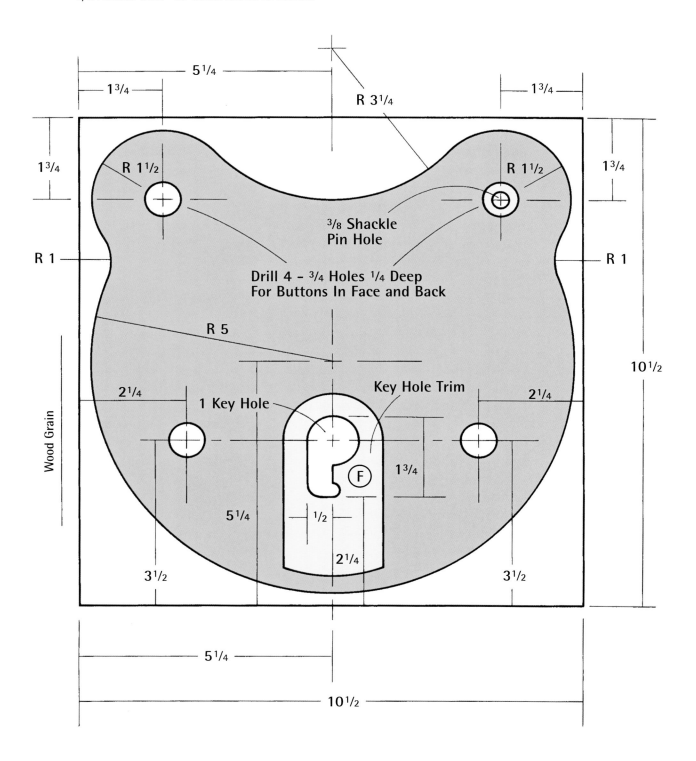

**Do Not Cut Lock To Shape until
Body Is Glued Together**

STEP # 1

Select the wood that you want to use for the front and backsides of the lock (Figure 29). Cut out two pieces exactly 10^1/$_2$ inches by 10^1/$_2$ inches from ^{3}/$_4$ inch thick material. These two pieces must be cut square and exactly the same size with vertical wood grain.

STEP # 2

Lay out the centers of the four, ^{3}/$_4$ inch holes for the wood buttons per Figure 30 on the face of the lock. Lay out the keyhole center and use Figure 35 to get the other dimensions needed. Use a compass to draw the shape of the face as in Figure 30. Be precise with your layout. Do not cut to shape now.

STEP # 3

Lay out the button hole centers on the back of the lock just as you did on the face in Step #2, but do not mark the keyhole. Drill ^{3}/$_4$ inch holes to a depth of ^{1}/$_4$ inch for the four buttons. Note: You need eight ^{3}/$_4$-inch wood buttons for the final assembly.

STEP # 4

Turn the back lamination over and use Figure 29 to mark the location of the lever pivot dowel and the key pivot dowel centers.

Use a ^{3}/$_8$ inch drill to drill these two holes ^{1}/$_2$ inch deep into the back lamination.

STEP # 5

Drill a 1 inch hole through the face lamination to make the top of the keyhole, Figure 30.

Now use a ^{1}/$_2$ inch drill bit to drill the bottom of the keyhole. If you use a Forstner bit, drill another ^{1}/$_2$ inch hole between this hole and the 1 inch hole.

Drill a ^{1}/$_4$ inch hole to the right of the first ^{1}/$_2$ inch hole as shown in Figure 35.

Carefully cut the rest of the keyhole out to shape with a chisel or knife and sand it smooth.

Lay the face lamination on the back lamination. The hole for the key pivot must be in the exact center of the keyhole.

STEP # 6

Cut a piece of ^{3}/$_8$ inch dowel 1^3/$_4$ inches long and glue it into the lever pivot hole. Cut a piece of ^{3}/$_8$ inch dowel 2^1/$_8$ inches long. Sand one end, rounding it over a little, and glue the other end into the key pivot hole.

STEP # 7

Use a ^{3}/$_4$ inch Forstner drill bit to drill all four button holes ^{1}/$_4$ inch deep in the face lamination.

STEP # 8

Drill a ^{3}/$_8$ inch hole all the way through the face lamination, see Figure 30, for the shackle retainer pin. This hole must be in the exact center of the ^{3}/$_4$ inch button hole recess (Photo 23).

Photo 23: All Holes Drilled in Lock Face

STEP #9

Figure 31 is the center lamination D of the lock body. It is made from a piece of wood 1¹/₂ inches thick and 10¹/₂ inches by 10¹/₂ inches square.

Be precise laying out this lamination. Check and double-check your layout. Please note the wood grain direction is vertical.

Cut along all lines with care because this piece becomes quite fragile. Do not cut the 3¹/₄ inch arc at the top now. It will be cut after the lock has been glued together, along with the rest of the outside shape of the lock.

Figure 31. (D) Body Center Lamination
1/2 Actual Size—all dimensions in inches

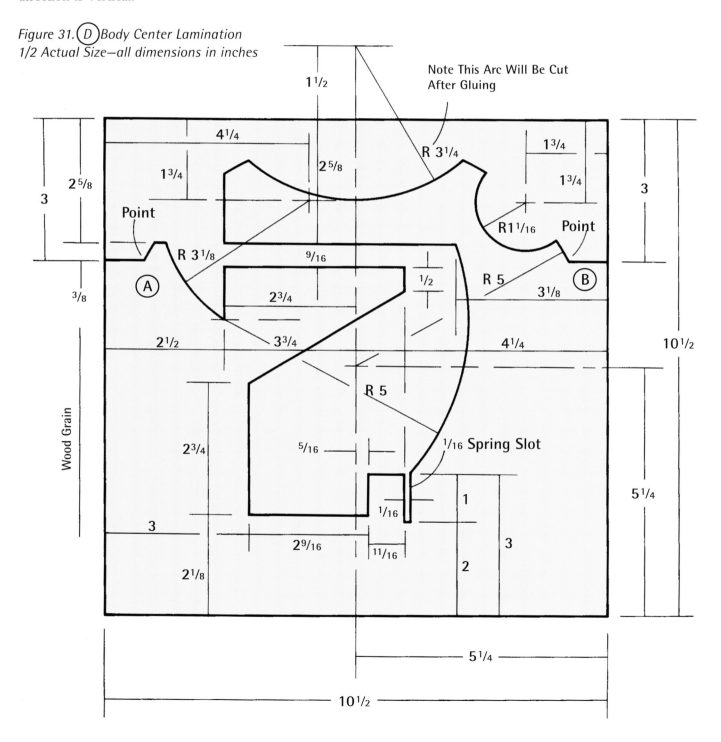

STEP #10

Sand the cutout portion of the center lamination from point A to point B, see Figure 31 and Photo 24.

Lay the face, the back and the center laminations aside for now.

STEP #11

The locking bolt B (Figure 32) should be made of a piece of hardwood. The spring notch is to be cut as shown in the front view so that the spring does not bind when the bolt is retracted.

Sand the entire bolt smooth. Sand the bottom of the tip of the bolt on the under side of the left end. See Figure 32 front view.

Photo 24: Center Lamination

Photo 25: Latch Bolt

Figure 32. (B) *Latch Bolt*
Actual Size—all dimensions in inches

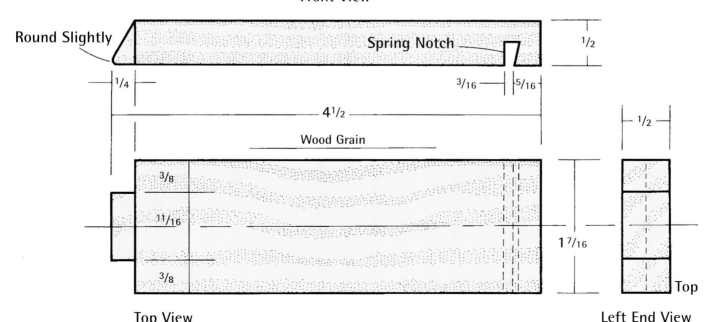

Front View

Round Slightly

Spring Notch ¹/₂

¹/₄ ³/₁₆ ⁵/₁₆

4¹/₂

Wood Grain

¹/₂

³/₈

¹¹/₁₆

³/₈

1⁷/₁₆

Top

Top View **Left End View**

STEP #12

The lever is also made of hardwood. Follow Figure 33 to make the lever. The lever must be about 1/16 inch thinner than the center lamination or 1 7/16 inches thick.

After the layout has been drawn on the wood, drill the 3/8 inch pivot hole.

Now saw out the rest of the lever and sand it smooth (Photo 26).

STEP #13

Make a flat wood spring of straight-grained ash or hickory. The spring is 1/16 inch thick, 1 1/4 inches wide and 5 1/2 inches long. Sand it smooth.

STEP #14

Glue the spring in the spring notch of the center lamination Figure 31. Make sure it will not rub on the lock face or back lamination when the lock is glued together.

STEP #15

Line up the three body laminations on the sides and bottom and clamp so that you can still lay the lock on the drill press.

Use a 3/8 inch wood bit and set the drill to drill only 1/2 inch into the back lamination. This hole must be drilled through the 3/8 inch hole that was drilled in the face lamination in Step #8. This is to make sure the hole is exactly straight in the lock.

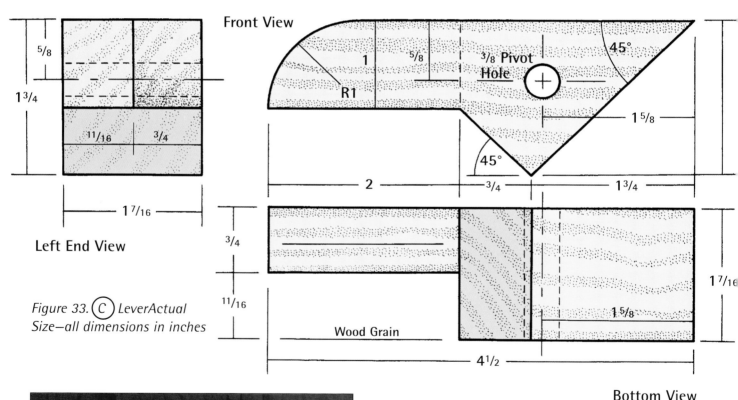

Figure 33. (C) Lever Actual Size—all dimensions in inches

Photo 26: Lever

STEP #16

Now check to see if the latch bolt and the lever fit properly (Photo 27).

Remove the face of the lock and lay in the latch bolt. It should slide back and forth in the bolt notch without binding. The spring must not bind when the bolt is pushed back. If the spring rests on the stop under the bolt, and the lever just touches the spring, you will not have to make adjustments. You may have to sand a little off the face of the lever that contacts the spring.

STEP #17

Draw a full size pattern on a sheet of paper of the shackle E as drawn in Figure 29. Make a horizontal line on the paper that goes through the center pivot point of the shackle. Draw the 3-inch radius inside of the shackle with a compass. Now draw the outside radius of $4^{1}/_{2}$ inches from the same point. The center of the retainer pinhole will be $1^{1}/_{2}$ inches below the horizontal line drawn for the pivot point.

Finish the layout of the pivot end of the shackle and then using Figure 34 layout the locking end of the shackle. Make sure to run the wood grain up and down as in Figure 29.

If you have not selected the wood for the shackle, do so now. It must be $^{1}/_{16}$ inch thinner than the center lock body lamination D when finished.

Use carbon paper to transfer the pattern of the shackle to the wood.

You can lay out the shackle directly on the wood if you like, but if you want to make another lock it is best to make a pattern for the shackle.

Carefully, cut out the shackle and then sand it smooth. Taper the latch end as in Figure 34 right side view.

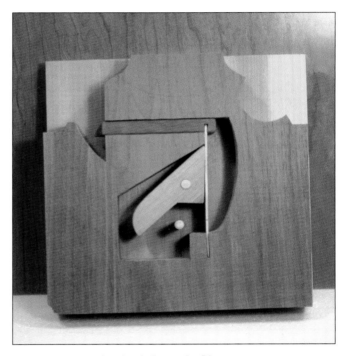

Photo 27 Interior Lock Parts in Place

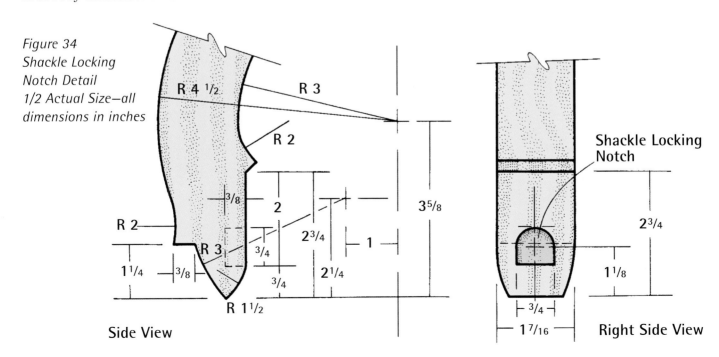

*Figure 34
Shackle Locking
Notch Detail
1/2 Actual Size—all
dimensions in inches*

R 4 1/2   R 3

R 2

R 2

R 3

3/8   2

2 3/4

1   3/4

1 1/4   3/8   3/4

2 1/4

3 5/8

R 1 1/2

Side View

Shackle Locking Notch

2 3/4

1 1/8

3/4

1 7/16

Right Side View

Photo 28: Completed Shackle

STEP #18 FITTING THE SHACKLE

Lay the center body lamination on the back lamination, and clamp together. Insert a ³/₈ inch by 3 inch dowel temporarily into the shackle pivot hole. Install the shackle on the pivot. The shackle must move freely on the pivot pin. If it does not, make the hole in the shackle just a little bigger.

Make sure the back and center laminations line up on both edges and the bottom. Try to close the shackle into the locked position. Check the fit everywhere. The two little peaks on the latch end of the shackle should rest on the center lamination, as in Figure 29. Fit as needed.

STEP #19

With the shackle closed, mark on the shackle end where the bottom of the latch bolt will hit it. This is the bottom of the locking notch to be cut, as in Figure 34. You can drill a hole or use a sharp chisel to cut the notch. The notch must be big enough to accept the end of the latch bolt.

Place the locking bolt and the lever in position and try to close the lock. You may have to do some fitting of the bolt and or the shackle notch to make the lock work properly. You should be able to push the shackle shut and lock the lock, and push the lever with your finger to retract the bolt and unlock the lock (Photo 28).

STEP #20

Gluing the Lock Body

Remove the clamps and take all the pieces apart.

Lay the back down and then apply glue to the back of the center lamination. Only use enough glue to do the job. Do not use excess glue because it will squeeze out and make spots in the finish. Make sure that NO glue will get on the locking bolt when the body has been clamped together, or your lock will be ruined. Carefully place the center lamination on the lock back. Line up the sides and bottom. Do not move it around or you will spread glue where you don't want it.

Place the latch bolt and the lever in position.

Spread glue on top of the center lamination, being very careful with the glue as in Step A.

Place the face lamination on top. Be careful not to slide it around.

Let the lock set a couple minutes and then start clamping it. Do not let any of the pieces slide around while clamping. Stick your finger in the top of the lock and make sure the latch bolt is still free to slide. If not, remove the lock face immediately, before the glue sets, and fix the problem.

STEP #21

While the glue dries in the lock body, go to Figure 35 to layout the keyhole trim piece F.

Cut and sand this piece of wood to approximately 1/8 inch in thickness.

Drill or cut out the keyhole so that the piece of 1 inch dowel you select for the key shaft will slip through it without binding. The keyhole trim should match the keyhole in the lock face. Round over all edges (except on the backside) with sandpaper.

STEP #22

Remove the clamps from the lock body and saw to the shape as described in Step #2. Saw carefully, so it will be easier to sand and smooth around the contour of the lock. Sand to make the curve around the lock as even as you can.

STEP #23

Round over the front and back edge of the lock body with a 3/8 inch round-over bit if you have one. If not, sand it round.

Round over both sides of the shackle from the points on the inside and outside of the latch end to the start of the 1 inch radius on the pivot end, also with the 3/8 inch round-over bit.

Figure 35. (F) *Key Hole Trim*
Actual Size—all dimensions in inches

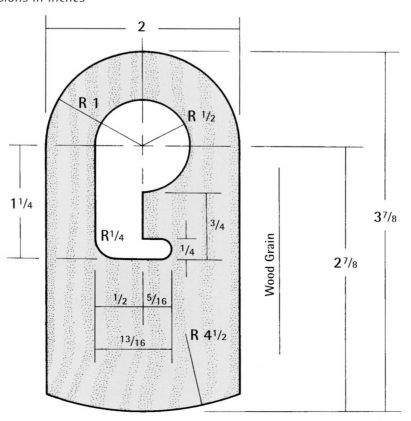

Figure 36. Key
Actual Size—all dimensions in inches

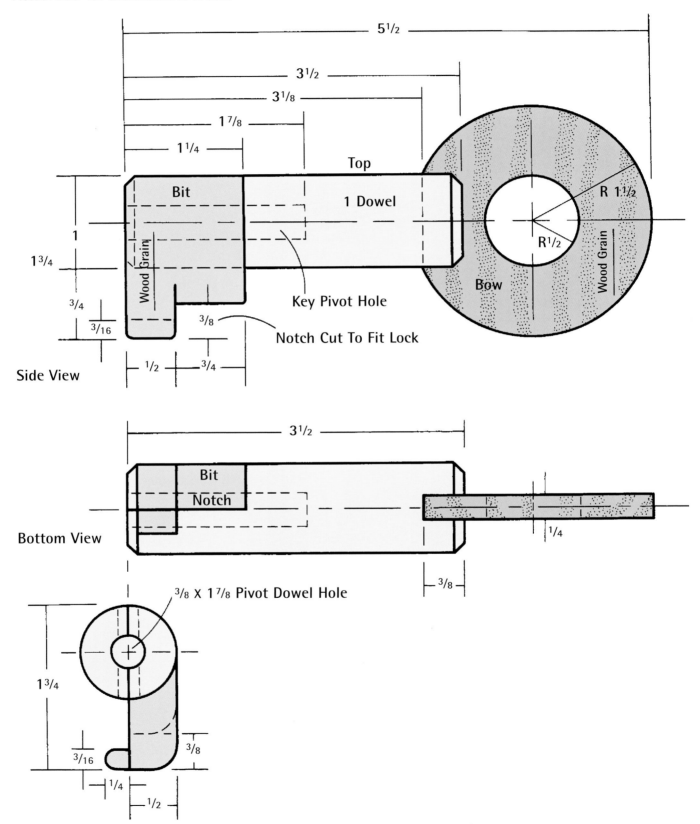

Side View

Bottom View

Left End View

STEP #24 THE KEY

1. Use Figure 36 while making the key. Cut a $3^1/2$ inch length of the 1 inch dowel you selected for the key shaft.

2. Cut the notch for the bit exactly half way, or $1/2$ inches, into the side of the shaft and $1^1/4$ inches from the end.

3. Cut a piece of wood $1/2$ inch thick, $1^1/4$ inches wide and $1^3/4$ inches long for the bit and glue it into place in the notch that you cut in the key shaft. Note the direction of the wood grain.

4. Make the key bow from $1/4$ inch thick wood. Use the pattern in Figure 36 or design one of your own. Cut to shape and sand smooth.

5. Mark the location of the bow notch on the end of the key shaft. Then carefully cut the notch just wide enough for the key bow to slip into place.

6. Before you glue the bow into place, drill the 3/8 inch pivot hole $1^7/8$ inch into the center of the bit end of the key. This hole must be absolutely straight and in the center. Try to put the key in the lock. You may have to enlarge the hole in the key.

7. Now glue the key bow in place with a small amount of glue.

8. Cut a small piece of wood for the small extension at the bottom of the key bit; see Figure 36 left end view. Glue in place on the bit as shown, and let dry.

9. Now cut the bit notch as shown. *Note: Only cut $1/8$ inch out at the start. Try the key in the lock. It must slide into the lock without binding. Now turn the key clockwise but do not use excessive force. The key should turn until it hits the stop that is built into the lever in the lock. You may have to cut the notch in the key deeper to allow the key to turn to the stop. Also round over the notch shown as a dotted line on the bit shown in the left end view in Figure 36. This allows the key to turn easily. Keep fitting the key until when the key is turned to the stop; the latch bolt is retracted just even with the shackle notch.

Photo 29: Key

STEP #25

Place the shackle in position and insert the 3/8 inch retainer dowel that you used when fitting the shackle into the pivot hole.

Close the shackle and snap it shut. Use the key to unlock and open the lock. Your lock should work with ease.

STEP #26

Sand all parts with the wood grain. Sand out all marks and scratches. Finish with 220-grit sandpaper. I cannot stress enough how important it is to sand the lock properly to prepare it for the finish.

STEP #27

Glue the keyhole trim in place with just enough glue. Do not let any glue squeeze out around the edges. Make sure the trim is straight and centered over the keyhole.

STEP #28

Prepare a place to hang the lock, shackle, and key after you apply the finish.

STEP #29

Clean all parts thoroughly with a vacuum cleaner and wipe off with a tack cloth.

I use polyurethane finish, but you can use the finish you prefer. I recommend you not spray the finish. If the finish runs into the shackle notch and gets on the latch bolt, it may ruin your lock.

Apply at least two coats of finish. Lightly sand with very fine sandpaper and clean as before to prepare for each additional coat of finish. Do not forget to finish the eight wood buttons.

STEP #30

Glue the four wood buttons in the holes in the back of the lock.

STEP #31

Place the shackle in position in the lock and insert the $3/8$ inch retainer pin. Mark the pin at the face of the lock. Remove the pin and cut $1/4$ inch shorter than the mark. Place a bead of glue on the end of the pin and insert all the way into the hole.

STEP #32

Glue the other four wood buttons into the holes in the face of the lock.

This completes the Giant Antique Lever Lock. I have made twenty-seven of these locks and each one is unique as no two wood projects can be exactly alike.

Photo 30: Finished Safe

Safe and Bank

This safe is of my design. It is the result of many people at art and craft shows asking if I had any boxes or lock boxes for sale.

Please read the text and familiarize yourself with the drawings before starting to make the safe.

First decide what wood you are going to use to make the safe. You need a minimum of 5 lineal feet of 1x8 to make the main body or box of the safe. You also need a 12-inch piece of 1x8 for the door. All pieces of the safe body must be flat and cannot be cupped or have a twist in them.

If you make the door of a contrasting colored wood, it makes a more attractive safe. The combination dial, hinges, and the bolt knob base should be made of the same wood as the safe body. The knob on the combination dial can be the same wood as the door.

Figure 37 is a key to the parts of the safe.

Figure 37.Safe and Bank Assembled Pieces (A) Through (E)
1/2 Actual Size—all dimensions in inches

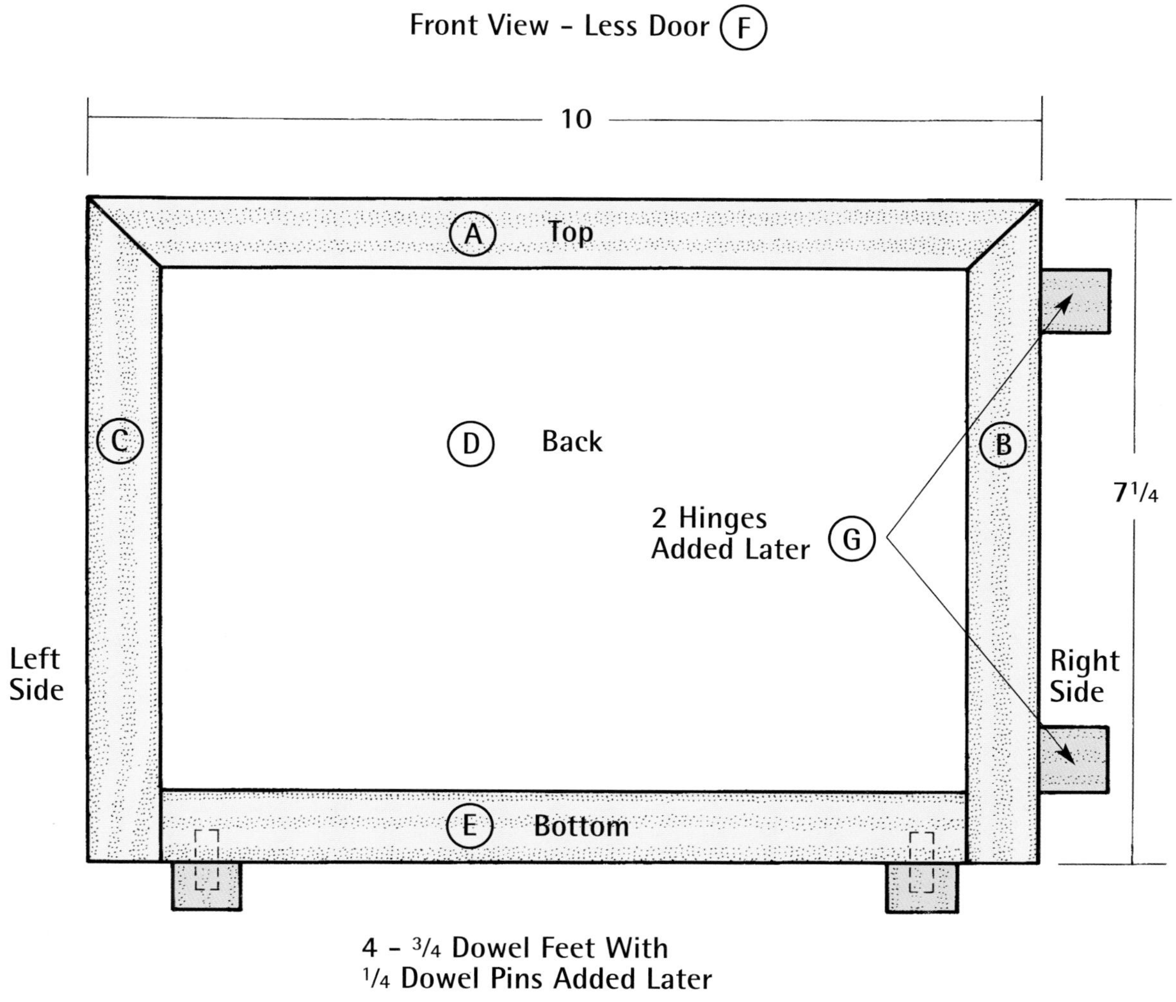
Front View - Less Door (F)
10
(A) Top
(C)
(D) Back
(B)
2 Hinges
Added Later (G)
7 1/4
Left
Side
Right
Side
(E) Bottom
4 - 3/4 Dowel Feet With
1/4 Dowel Pins Added Later

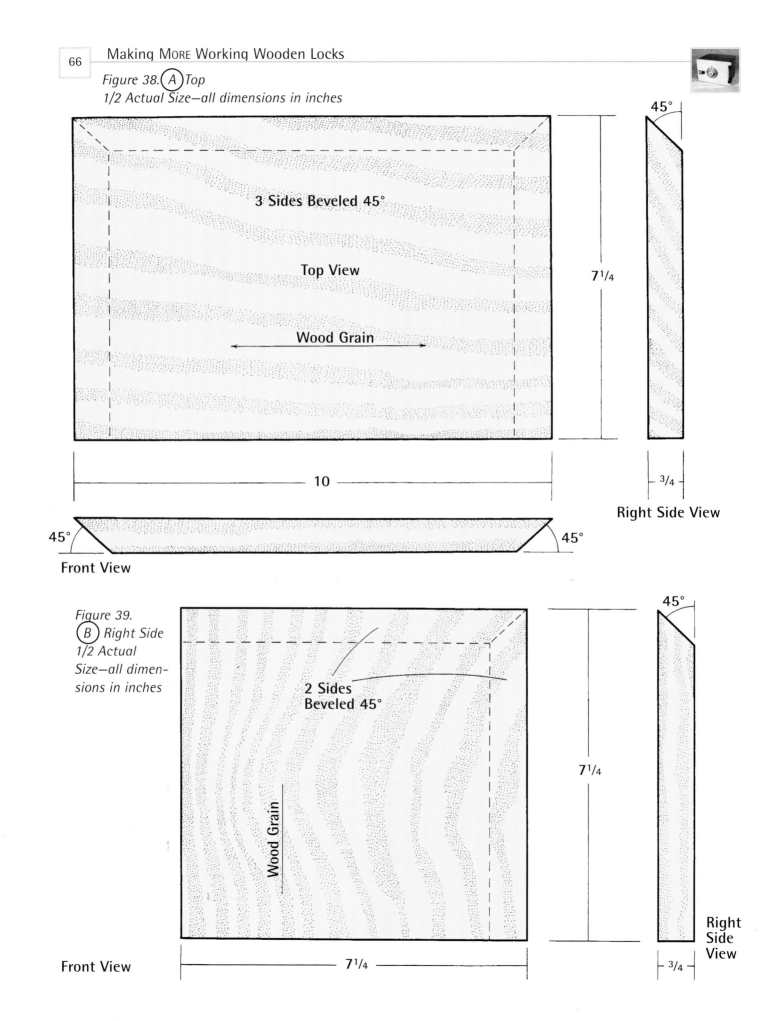

Figure 38. (A) Top
1/2 Actual Size—all dimensions in inches

3 Sides Beveled 45°

Top View

Wood Grain

7¼

45°

Right Side View

¾

10

45°   45°

Front View

Figure 39.
(B) Right Side
1/2 Actual
Size—all dimen-
sions in inches

2 Sides
Beveled 45°

45°

7¼

Wood Grain

Front View   7¼

Right
Side
View

¾

STEP #1

Make the top A of the safe as in Figure 38. Make all cuts precisely as indicated. The top must be exactly square and the three edges cut exactly on a 45-degree bevel.

STEP #2

The right side of the safe B is made from Figure 39.

STEP #3

Make the left side of the safe C as in Figure 40. Use a ³/₄ inch Forstner bit to drill the bolt hole ¹/₂ inch deep into the back or inside of this piece.

Figure 40. (C) Left Side
1/2 Actual Size—all dimensions in inches

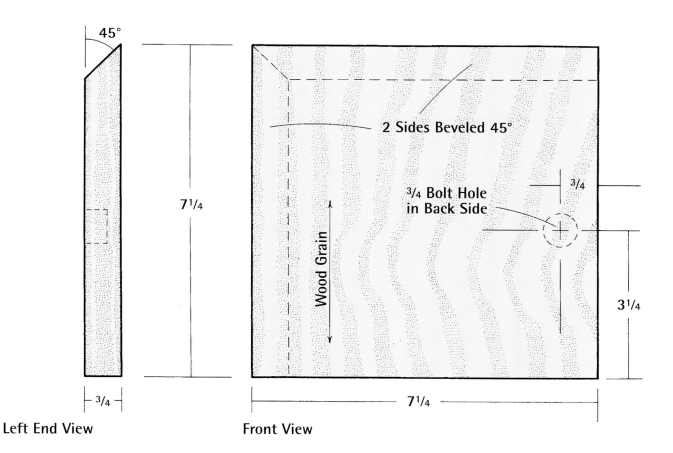

Figure 41. (D) *Back - Same As Top* (A)
Except Coin Slot in Top edge of Back
All dimensions in inches

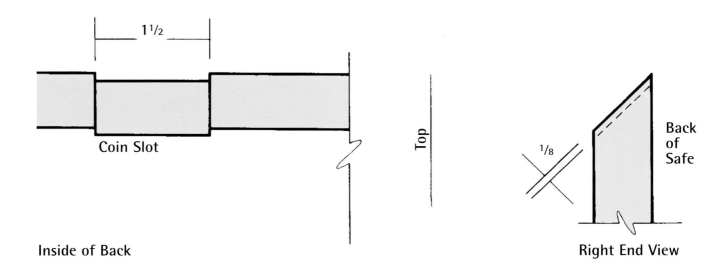

1¹/₂

Coin Slot

Inside of Back

Top

¹/₈

Back
of
Safe

Right End View

Figure 42. (E) *Bottom*
1/2 Actual Size—all dimensions in inches

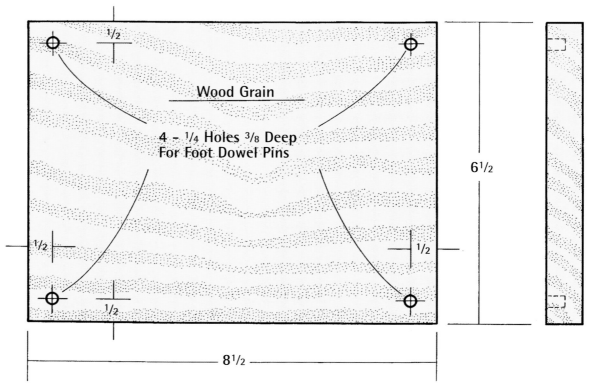

¹/₂

Wood Grain

4 - ¹/₄ Holes ³/₈ Deep
For Foot Dowel Pins

¹/₂

¹/₂

¹/₂

6¹/₂

8¹/₂

Bottom View

Right End View

STEP #4

The back of the safe D is made exactly the same shape and size as the top A was made in Step #1, Figure 38. If you want to make a coin slot in the bank, use Figure 41 to cut the coin slot in the top edge of the back.

STEP #5

Cut out the bottom of the safe as in Figure 42. All cuts and edges must be square. Drill the four holes for the foot dowel pins ³/₈ inch deep into the bottom or on the outside of the bottom.

STEP #6

Trial fit the safe sides, top and bottom together to check the fit of all joints and miters. If they fit, place the bottom on a flat surface and glue the right side B and left side C in place and then clamp them. Check to make sure they are square to the bottom.

STEP #7

Glue the top A in place and clamp it so the miters fit on both ends. The safe body must be square and have no twist.

STEP #8

Glue the safe back D in place. Again make sure all joints and miters fit (Photo 31).

Photo 31: Safe Body Glued Together

STEP #9

Place the safe door, Figure 43, on the front of the safe. Line up the top, left side and the bottom. Do whatever is necessary to make it fit. The door should be about 1 inch past the right side of the safe. Mark along the right side on the back of the door. This is where the door must be cut to fit.

Now remove the door and lay out the hinges on the top and bottom as in Figure 43. Cut very carefully along the lines leaving just enough wood for sanding.

Mark the centers of the hinge pin holes on the top and bottom of the door, but do not drill them now.

STEP #10

Lay out the center of the dial anchor plate hole and the hole for the locking bolt knob hole on the face of the door as in Figure 43.

Drill the 2$^{1}/_{8}$ inch hole for the anchor plate all the way through the door.

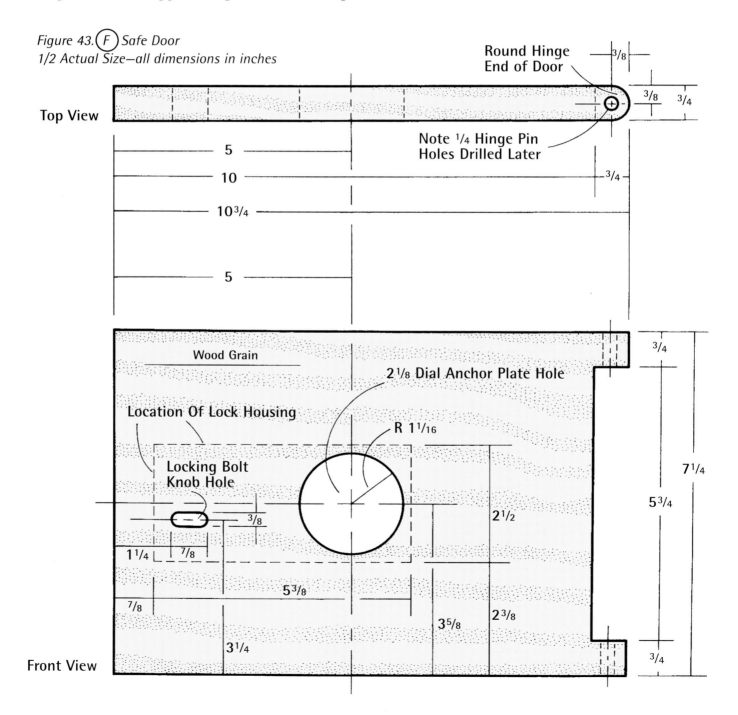

Figure 43. (F) *Safe Door*
1/2 Actual Size—all dimensions in inches

STEP #11

The lock housing, Figure 44, is made from a solid block of wood or it can be a glued up block. Cut the block to shape and sand smooth on all sides. Mark the center of the $1^7/_8$ inch tumbler hole.

Place on your drilling platform, and bore out the tumbler hole to a depth of $1^3/_8$ inches. Do not move the platform. Now change to a $^1/_4$ inch Forstner bit, and bore a hole for the tumbler post exactly in the center of the tumbler hole to within $^1/_8$ inch of the drilling platform, see Figure 44.

Figure 44. Lock Housing
Actual Size—all dimensions in inches

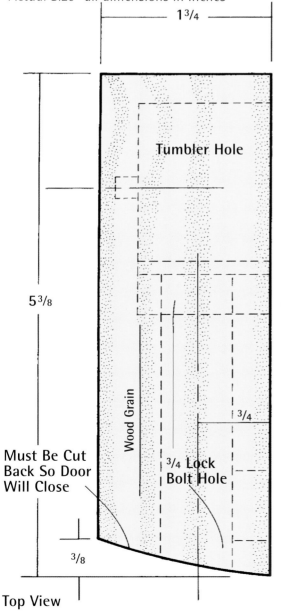

Top View

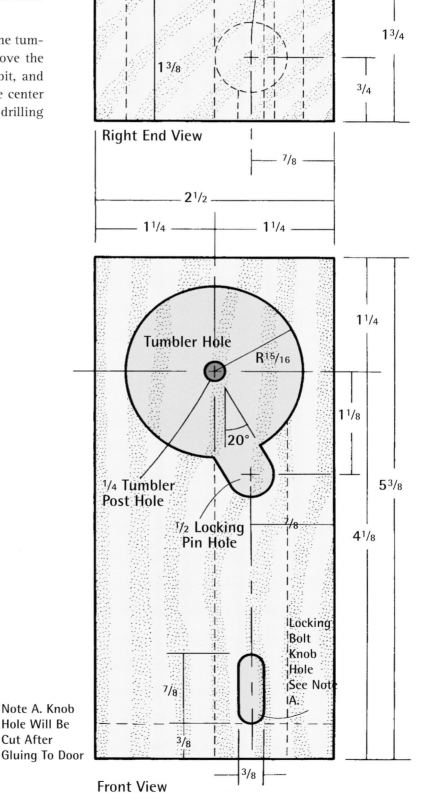

Front View

STEP #12

Mark the center location of the locking pin hole, Figure 44, on the tumbler block. Use a $1/2$ inch Forstner bit to bore the hole exactly the same depth as the tumbler hole.

Use a sharp chisel to cut the rest of the locking pin-hole. This hole must be cut as shown in the Figure 44 front view.

STEP #13

Locate and mark the center of the lock bolt hole on the left end of the lock housing $7/8$ inch from the bottom and $3/4$ inch from the front. Clamp the lock housing to the drilling platform and position to drill the $3/4$ inch lock bolt hole. This hole must be absolutely straight and parallel with the lock housing. Drill all the way into the tumbler hole. Now use a knife and sandpaper to remove all slivers and rough places. Sand the entire housing smooth and round the corners slightly (Photo 32).

Photo 32: Finished Lock Housing

STEP #14

Sand the back of the safe door smooth and then position the lock housing as shown in Figure 43, on the inside or back of the door. When in position there should be a 1/8 inch ledge all the way around inside the anchor plate hole in the door. The bolt hole end of the lock housing should be 7/8 inch back from the left edge of the door. If everything is in the correct position, lightly mark the location of the housing and then glue it to the door. Clamp it in place, but do not let it move on the door.

STEP #15

The bolt knob, Figure 45, is used to retract the locking bolt after the combination has been dialed. Make the knob with the same kind of wood as you used for the safe body. If you like you can make a knob of your design, just make sure the base of the knob is at least 2 inches long, as this will cover the hole in the door when the bolt is moved.

Figure 45. Bolt Knob
Actual Size—all dimensions in inches

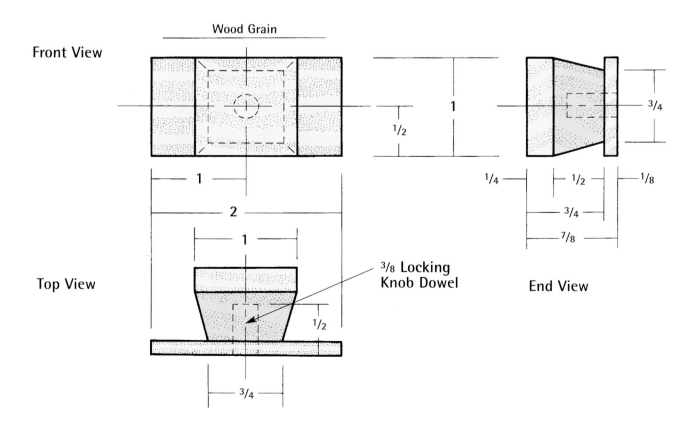

STEP #16

Use Figure 46 to make two hinges. I like to use the same wood as for the safe body. Make exactly as shown but do not drill the hinge pin holes now. The drawings only show where the holes will be. Sand smooth on all sides and edges.

STEP #17

Lay the safe on its back and place the door on top. Line the door up on all sides. If it does not fit, you need to sand and fit it now.

When the door fits properly, clamp it in place. Be careful when clamping so as not to mar the wood.

Now turn the safe and lay it on its left side. Place the two hinges that were made in Step #16 in place between the hinge projections on the door. Place them against the door hinges and parallel with the top and bottom of the safe. The round end of the hinges should match the round ends on the door. When lined up, make very small marks on the safe body to mark the location. Put just enough glue on the back of the loose hinge to glue it to the side of the safe. Do not use excess glue so it does not squeeze out. Let dry completely. Do not remove the clamps.

Figure 46. (G) Hinge - 2 Required
Actual Size—all dimensions in inches

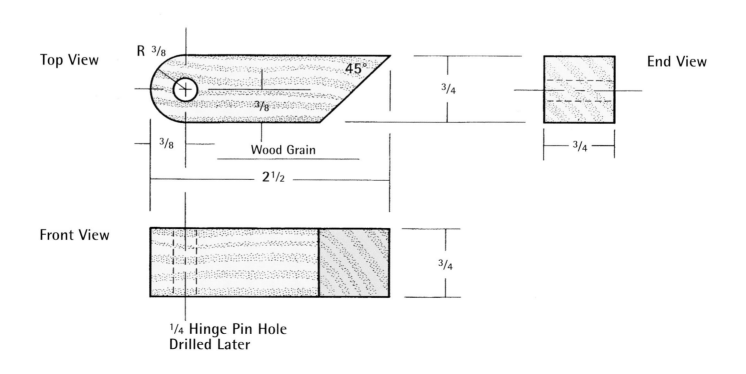

STEP #18

When the hinges are dry, mark the centers of the hinge pin holes on the top of the top hinge and the bottom of the bottom hinge. Be precise, because the pins must be centered so the hinge will not bind when the door is opened.

With the door still clamped in place, use a ¼ inch bit in your drill press to drill absolutely straight through both hinges at the top and bottom. Remove the clamps and the safe door.

STEP #19

Make a small mark on each hinge on the right side of the safe, 1³/₈ inches from the round or pivot end and ³/₈ inch from the top, to center a ¼ inch hole. Drill these holes 1¼ inches deep through the hinge and into the safe side.

Cut two pieces of ¼ inch dowel 1 inch long, spread a little glue on each dowel, and push them all the way into each hole. This anchors the hinges in place so they will not break loose when the door is opened.

Make wood plugs from the same wood as the hinges and glue them in the holes. When dry, cut and sand the plugs flush with the surface of the hinges.

STEP #20

The dial anchor plate, Figure 47, is used to glue the dial and the drive tumbler into the door in final assembly.

The anchor plate should be just small enough to slip into the hole in the door. Please note the thickness, as the anchor plate should protrude approximately ¹/₁₆ inch outside the face of the door so that the combination dial does not rub on the door when it is turned.

Figure 47. Dial Anchor Plate
Actual Size—all dimensions in inches

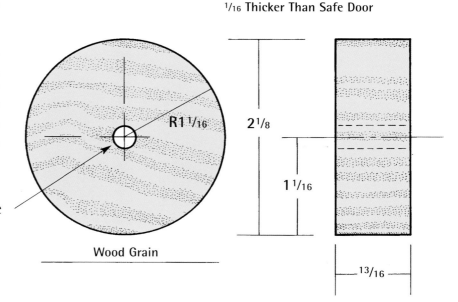

Anchor Plate Must Be
¹/₁₆ Thicker Than Safe Door

R1 ¹/₁₆   2¹/₈

1 ¹/₁₆

¼ **Pivot Hole**

Wood Grain

¹³/₁₆

STEP #21

Use a 3/4 inch dowel to make the locking bolt. See Figure 48. Cut a piece of dowel 4 inches long.

The locking bolt must slide freely in the bolt hole of the lock housing. Do not cut the ends to shape yet.

STEP #22

Now make the hole in the door for the locking bolt knob, Figure 43. This hole must be centered vertically on the locking bolt hole. Drill a 3/8 inch hole at each end of the knob hole, then cut the rest of the hole out with a chisel. Cut carefully so a 3/8 inch dowel will slide left and right with just a little extra play in it.

STEP #23

Slide the 3/4 inch bolt into the housing and let the bolt protrude so it is even with the edge of the door on the left. Make a small thin wedge to put in the bolt hole beside the bolt so it wedges the bolt tight in the hole. It must not move while drilling.

STEP #24

Set up your drill press so you can drill a 3/8 inch hole at the left end of the locking knob hole that you made in the door in Step #22. Drill this hole 1/2 inch into the locking bolt, not through it, using the hole in the door as a guide.

After the hole has been drilled remove the bolt from the hole and clean the hole and the bolt of sawdust and chips.

Figure 48. Locking Bolt
Actual Size—all dimensions in inches

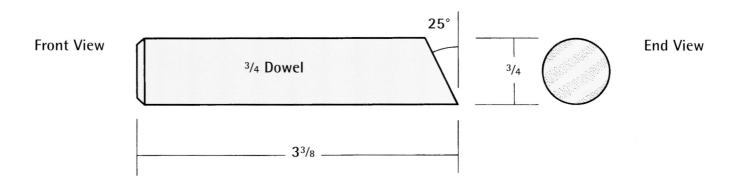

Front View   25°   End View

3/4 Dowel   3/4

3 3/8

Slide the bolt back in the bolt hole and place a piece of $3/8$ inch dowel in the hole that you just drilled. You must be able to move the bolt back and forth freely.

Move the bolt to the left or away from the tumbler hole, and make a mark on the bolt around the edge of the locking pin hole.

Now move the bolt to the right as far as it will go. The 3/8 inch dowel should be against the right end of the knob hole. Make a mark around the bolt where it goes into the lock housing at the edge of the housing.

Remove the bolt from the door. Cut off at the mark around the left end. Round the edges about $1/8$ inch.

Now look at Figure 48, and mark the 25-degree angle at the left edge of the mark you made in the locking pin hole.

Make sure you cut straight through the bolt from front to back. Sand smooth and round the edges over slightly. Lay the bolt aside until final assembly.

STEP #25

The best way to round the edges of the door is to clamp the lock housing in a bench vise, allowing you to rout around the edge of the door. I use a $5/16$ inch roundover bit to round mine. Look at Figure 43. Round over the $5^3/4$ inches between the hinge extensions only to the hinges. Do not round where the hinges come together with the hinges on the safe.

STEP #26

Use the $5/16$ inch round-over bit to round over all corners and edges of the safe body and door except where the door and safe body come together when the door is closed (Photo 33).

STEP #27

This is a good time to check the latch bolt operation. Place the door in position on the safe and temporarily insert a 2 inch length of $1/4$ inch dowel in the two hinges. The door should be even with the safe body all around the edges. The hinge pins are probably tight. They will be fitted in final assembly.

Open the door and slide the locking bolt into the bolt-hole. Place a 2 inch piece of $3/8$ inch dowel in the knob hole and into the hole in the bolt.

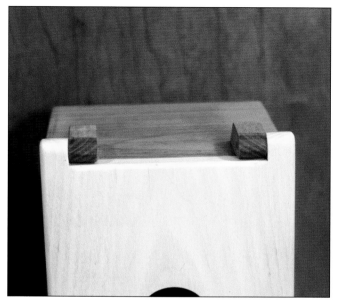

Photo 33: Hinges on Safe Body

Shut the safe door and slide the bolt to the left. If you cannot lock the door, find the reason, and start making adjustments until the bolt works properly. When the bolt is seated in the locked position, the angled end to the right should be even with the left side of the locking pin hole in the tumbler hole. See Figure 44.

STEP #28 THE DIAL

I prefer to make the dial from the same kind of wood the safe body is made of. Cut a piece of wood $3/8$ inch thick, and $3^3/4$ inches square (Figure 49). Make the knob of the same kind of wood as the safe door.

Saw the dial round as in Figure 49. Saw the knob from $3/4$ inch wood approximately $1^1/2$ inches in diameter. Glue the knob in the exact center of the dial. After the glue is dry, fasten to a small lathe faceplate exactly in the center. Carefully turn down the dial and knob. The final dial should be $3^1/2$ inches to $3^3/4$ inches in diameter. Round the edges on the face to your liking, and sand to at least 220-grit sandpaper to remove all scratches.

Figure 49. Dial
Actual Size—all dimensions in inches

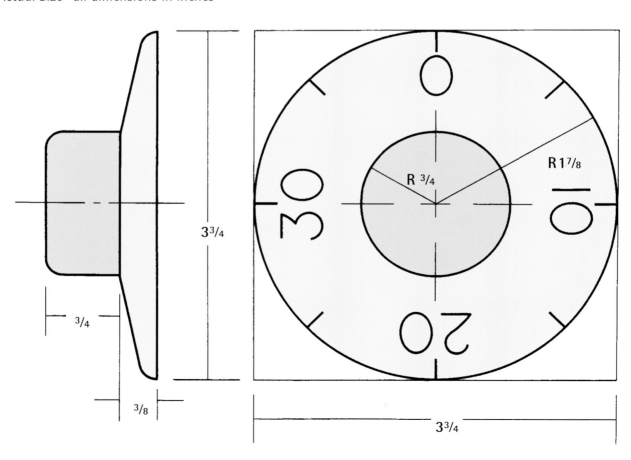

STEP #29

Remove the dial from the faceplate and lay out the small indicator marks around the rim of the dial every 45 degrees, as in Figure 49. I use a wood burner to do this but you can carve little notches or paint the marks on the dial.

Next you must put the numbers on. Again, I use a wood burner, but you can carve or paint them. You may want to use a number template, if you have one available, to help with layout.

STEP #30

Find the exact center on the back of the dial. Using a 1/4 inch bit in the drill press, drill 7/8 inch into the dial and knob. This hole must be perpendicular to the surface.

STEP #31

Using a piece of paper, very carefully lay out a pattern from the drawing of the three tumblers in Figure 50, 51, and 52.

Transfer the patterns onto pieces of 1/4 inch plywood. If you can get plywood 7/32 inch thick, use that type. The location of the locking pin notch and the drive pins must be exact or the combination will be changed.

Figure 50. Tumbler 1
Actual Size—all dimensions in inches

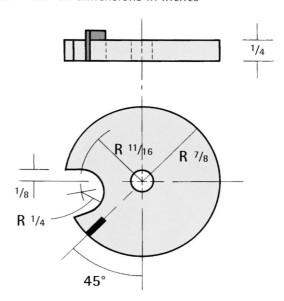

Figure 52. Tumbler 3
Actual Size—all dimensions in inches

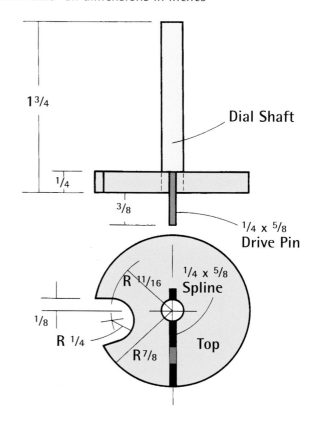

Figure 51. Tumbler 2
Actual Size—all dimensions in inches

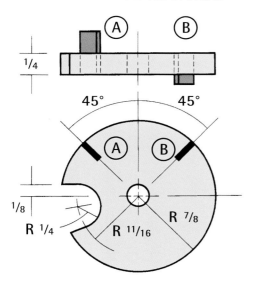

Photo 34: Finished Tumbler #1

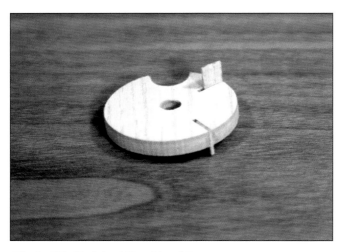

Photo 35: Finished Tumbler #2

Carefully cut out the tumblers. Mark the number of the tumbler and the top of each tumbler.

STEP #32

Drill the pivot hole with a $1/4$ inch drill exactly in the center of each tumbler.

STEP #33

Now saw the drive pin notches on a band saw. One saw cut should be enough, approximately $1/16$ inch wide.

When sawing the drive pin notch in Tumbler #3 (Figure 52), saw in a straight-line $1/8$ inch beyond the pivot hole in the center.

STEP #34

Next cut the locking pin notch in each tumbler using a scroll saw or a band saw with a $1/8$ inch blade.

STEP #35

Pick a piece of straight fine grained ash or hickory (my favorite), and saw or sand down a spline to fit the cuts in the tumblers, $1/16$ inch thick and $1/4$ inch wide. You only need enough to make five pieces approximately $1/2$ inch long; so, make 5 inches or 6 inches of spline this size. I use a sharp tin snips to cut the pieces to length as needed. You can use a knife or fine-toothed saw.

STEP #36

Start with Tumbler #1 (Figure 50). Cut a $1/2$ inch piece of spline, and glue it flush with the underside and the outside edge into the notch in Tumbler #1. Wipe the extra glue off and lay aside to dry (Photo 34).

STEP #37

For Tumbler #2 cut two pieces of spline $1/2$ inch long. Glue one into the notch lettered A in Figure 51, flush with the bottom and outside edge. Glue the other into the notch lettered B in Figure 51, flush with the top and the outside edge. Wipe extra glue off and set aside to dry (Photo 35).

STEP #38

For Tumbler #3 you need to cut a piece of $1/4$ inch dowel $1^3/_4$ inches long for the dial shaft (see Figure 52). Using the same saw that you cut the drive pin notches with, make a cut exactly centered into one end of the dial shaft, $1/4$ inch deep. Cut a piece of spline about $5/_8$ inch long and glue into the notch that you just cut in the dial shaft. Let only $1/_8$ inch of spline stick out from one side and the rest out the other side. Cover the spline and a little of the shaft with glue and insert into the top of the Tumbler #3. Make sure that the shaft is exactly perpendicular to the tumbler face, and flush with the underside. Place the tumbler over the edge of a table or board and roll back and forth with your finger to see if the tumbler wobbles. If it does, straighten the shaft. If it is not straight, the dial will wobble when the lock is finished. Remove all extra glue from the tumbler.

Cut another piece of spline $5/_8$ inch long and glue into the notch, flush with the top of the tumbler. Remove all extra glue, and set aside to dry (Photo 36).

Photo 36: Finished Tumbler #3

STEP #39

Cut four pieces of $3/4$ inch dowel $1/2$ inch or $3/4$ inch long for the feet under the safe.

Drill a $1/4$ inch hole half way through each foot in the center. Sand the other end of the foot smooth and round over the edge slightly.

Glue one of the $1/4$ inch dowels in each foot and let it protrude $1/4$ inch. The feet will be installed at final assembly (Photo 37).

STEP #40

If the door is on the safe, remove it. On the face of the door mark the center of a $1/4$ inch dowel location, 2 inches above the center of the tumbler hole. Drill a hole $1/4$ inch deep and glue a dowel of contrasting wood in the hole, cut off, and sand smooth. This is the combination reference point.

Proceed to sand the entire safe body, the door, dial, bolt knob, and the feet. Sand with the wood grain.

Work carefully and do not hurry this job. As in all projects the sanding and finish is what makes a beautiful final project.

Photo 37: Safe Feet

STEP #41 FINISHING

Prepare a place to put the parts to dry after the finish is applied.

Vacuum clean all parts and wipe with a tack cloth.

I like to apply polyurethane finish with a foam rubber brush, however, you may use your favorite finish and method of application.

Apply a minimum of two coats of finish. Sand lightly and clean between coats.

When all finish is dry, install the four feet on the safe. Put glue in each hole and push the feet into place. Wipe off any glue that may squeeze out.

STEP #42

Now find a $1/4$ inch dowel that will just go into the tumbler post hole (Figure 44). Cut a piece $1^1/4$ inches long and put some glue on the end. Insert it into the post hole and make sure it is all the way in and that

Figure 53. Dial Assembly

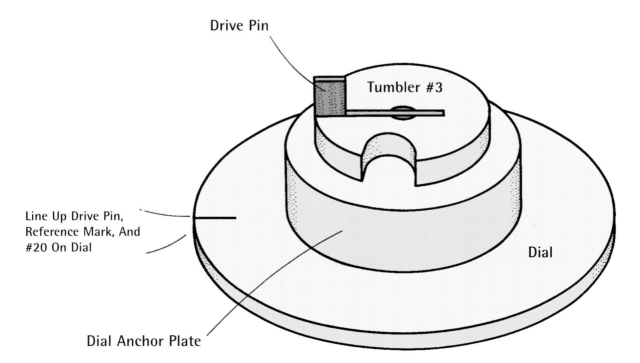

STEP #52

The combination:

1. Turn the dial counter clockwise three times to #5.

2. Turn the dial clockwise two times to #25.

3. Turn the dial counter clockwise one time to #0.

4. Open the safe. It should open very easily. If not, remove the dial assembly to see if the notches in the tumblers are in the right position. If there is a problem, it usually is Tumbler #2. Try the combination again. This time use the numbers 5-26-0. You may have to add or subtract one number at a time to any of the numbers. Each time, remove the dial to check the position of the notches. Remember the bottom Tumbler #1 goes counter clockwise, and the top Tumbler #2 goes clockwise.

The third number can be checked by reading the number on the dial when the lock is open with the dial in place.

You probably know now why I stressed accurate layout and cutting. A lot of different things can change the combination a little.

Once you have the combination, work the lock several times to be sure that it always works.

Now that the lock works to your satisfaction, open the lock, pull the bolt back and leave it open. Remove the dial assembly, and run a small bead of glue around the ledge for the anchor plate, and lay in the dial assembly.

Try the lock one more time, before the glue sets.

Congratulations!

You have made something that will be a gift of love, and a family heirloom to be a hand-me-down to children and grandchildren.

Gallery of Wooden Locks

Photo 42: Ohio Combination Lock

Photo 43: Push Key Pin Tumbler Lock

Photo 44: Melted Purple Heart Lock

Photo 45: Smokehouse Door Lock

Photo 46: 23" Mortise Lock with Over 90 Pieces of Wood

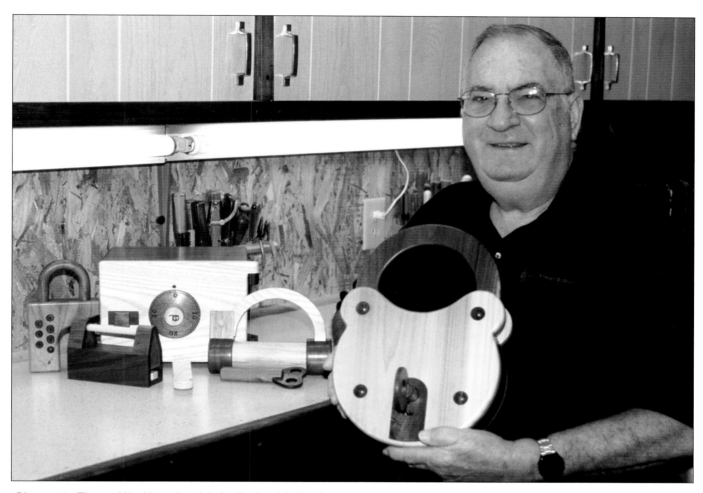

Photo 48: Tim at Workbench with Locks in this Book